HOUSING IN SCANDINAVIA

HOUSING
IN SCANDINAVIA

URBAN AND RURAL

BY JOHN GRAHAM, JR.

CHAPEL HILL

THE UNIVERSITY OF NORTH CAROLINA

PRESS · 1940

KINGSPORT PRESS, INC., KINGSPORT, TENNESSEE

To my wife
ELIZABETH GRAHAM
*who does more than her share
in every adventure.*

PREFACE

"THE QUESTION THAT BOTHERS ME IS THIS: IF WE give new housing with its sanitary plumbing and heating to the low income groups, won't we be whetting their appetites for more and more? . . . Isn't it establishing a dangerous precedent?"

The inquiry was addressed to the guest speaker, a prominent housing official, and came from one of a group of public-spirited citizens gathered around a dinner table discussing preliminary plans for the building of a public housing project in their city. In answer the guest speaker cited the experience of some of the European countries, saying that in the public housing of England, Holland, Denmark, Sweden, and other democracies the occupants had not been fired with avaricious designs. On the contrary, the people seemed appreciative and satisfied with their better living conditions, and he felt that in the light of this successful experience there was no reason to expect different results in the United States.

The question was a good one—good in the sense that it embodied the doubt and fear which so often oppress the mind of the average layman contemplating the amelioration of some social ill. Little did the questioner realize that he was echoing an age-old apprehension. "If we give the people *this*, won't they want *that*" has been the disturbing query down through the centuries. In the time of Tiberius a Roman senator rises and asks: "If we let the people elect the magistrates, won't they demand the election of other officials?" Centuries later Lord North asks his cabinet, "If we waive our parliamentary right of taxation, won't the colonists insist upon other privileges?" An ever-present question, dangerous to those forms of government that are tinged with absolutism but not properly disturbing to a democracy where the people decide what services shall be rendered.

Democracy in a pioneer society composed of comparatively few settlers in the midst of an abundance of natural resources becomes highly individualistic and will flourish under this rugged characteristic so long as the resources remain plentiful and there are few to exploit them. Chisholm, the cattle king of Texas, at the height of his prosperity was reported to have been the owner of a million acres of grazing ground. He exercised the prerogative of the pioneer by taking what was available through his own initiative and he was not to be blamed in that period. But let the pioneer period advance, the settlers multiply, the resources dwindle and then what an individual takes is not necessarily what is available but what may be a necessity for someone else. Then the end of the pioneer stage is at hand.

Fortunately democracy is flexible. Like a well-tempered toledo blade it can change its direction without breaking. For this one reason alone it is preferable to other forms of government such as autocracy, the tyrannical rule of one; oligarchy, the rigid rule of a few; or, it might be added, even to "partocracy," the stupid rule of party. Democracy, contrary to the desires of some, cannot remain in a state of repose. In its evolution it may be said to have three stages: the pioneer, the transitional, and the social. Whether we are aware of it or whether we regret it, the United States has outgrown the pioneer stage with its few people and readily available resources and is now passing through the transitional stage. And for its very existence it must perforce move into the social stage which, from the root to the flower, marks its maturity.

In the face of menacing world disorder today this country is confronted with the challenge: Can we make democracy work? We are apt to boast that the American standard of living is the highest in the world, and yet at the same time ignore the fact that almost one third of the nation has little or no standard of living. We shout "Liberty, everyone has liberty," forgetting that for a substantial number of our people the words in reality mean liberty to starve because of malnutrition, to suffer because of the lack of warm clothing, and to sicken because of bad housing. In a democracy liberty is more than a mere academic expression; it means affording access to the essentials of decent living for all. The story is told of a traveler to Norway centuries ago who approached a Viking and asked him, "Who is your chief?" The Viking proudly replied, "There is no chief. We are all chiefs here!" Equality becomes a part of democracy when the essentials of decent living are humanely distributed.

In the journey toward a dynamic and mature democracy, Denmark, Sweden, Norway, and Finland have already entered the social stage. Here we see vigorous efforts being made to achieve a more satisfying life for all groups of society. Particularly is this true in the field of social housing for the lower and medium income groups. Here the term "social housing" is employed to include those forms of housing where the social motive functions alone, where it predominates, or where it is mixed with the profit motive in varying degrees. In the municipalities we find various types of social housing: municipal apartments for the lowest income group, "self-help" housing for workers, co-operative and other public utility forms for the low and middle income groups, and industrial housing for the workers in industry. And as a base for this diversified housing is the intelligent conception of the social use of land.

In these countries before the World War it was realized that private enterprise, concerned entirely with the profit motive, had been unable to supply the housing needs of the poorer groups who could not meet the rents demanded for suitable dwellings. There were only two ways of improving the existing living conditions. One was to increase substantially the purchasing power of the worker, and the other was to lower materially the rent of dwellings; the first was impossible to bring about, therefore the second course was adopted and the government intervened in the housing field. Besides the direct advantages gained by the low income groups securing better living conditions, public activity had the important effect of centering national attention on the housing problem which previously had been generally neglected.

Concerning the problem of rural housing in the four Scandinavian countries, emphasis has been placed on the truism that no solution exists apart from the interrelated factors of improved agricultural living and income. Consequently, these countries have engaged in an extensive and far-reaching program of creating small farm holdings for the maintenance of an independent rural population. The government-directed programs of securing available land and dividing large properties into small independent and semi-independent farms are re-establishing the man on the soil. It is a convincing answer to the land question and farm tenancy. It is an escape from those forces which brought land serfdom to Hellenistic Greece, to Rome of the latifundia, to Europe of the feudalistic middle ages. As a Danish educator describes it, "The small holder movement has become one of the best elements in the development of the last few generations: the demand for equal rights for all to the national land and the necessity for co-operation. The more we share progress with our neighbors, the better for all; the more thoroughly the individual home does its work, the better will be the common result. Can the prosperity of a nation be based on a sounder foundation?"

Housing constitutes but one phase of the many social accomplishments which characterize the Scandinavian democracies. Nearly forty-five years ago Denmark became the first country to establish old-age pensions on a voluntary basis with government aid. Sweden, without placing reliance upon antitrust legislation, controls monopolies through co-operative societies operated by the people. Finland, within the span of one short generation, has performed the feat of bringing its rural population out of a backward agricultural position into successful competition for world markets. Strong organizations of employers and employees are recognized by these governments as the instruments for orderly collective bargaining. Furthermore, with government financial assistance, extensive workers' education is being sponsored by the trades unions and other organizations in urban centers. In rural areas, the people's colleges and small holder schools are building an enlightened citizenship.

While every effort has been made to present faithfully facts, figures, and observations in this book, if by chance any inaccuracies occur the writer takes refuge behind one of Dr. Samuel Johnson's celebrated replies. When asked by a lady, with degree of intent to confound, why he defined in his dictionary the word "pastern" as "the *knee* of a horse," he solemnly answered, "From ignorance, madam, pure ignorance."

JOHN GRAHAM, JR.

"Burnswark,"
New Hope, Pennsylvania
August 12, 1939

ACKNOWLEDGMENTS

TO THE READER ABOUT TO DIP INTO A BOOK AN AR-
ray of acknowledgments often appears formidable and, like haz-
ards on a golf course, seem placed in one's path merely to delay
progress. An author, however, in justice both to his feeling of gratitude, and in a lesser degree his vanity, cannot readily omit this
part of the foreword. Acknowledgments are bread and butter
notes pressed into a small package and inserted in recognition of
valuable assistance received. Also they lend a touch of impres-
siveness to a book which is not without advantage in an age when
to "blush unseen" is looked upon as a master crime. Among the
many in Scandinavia who generously contributed their time and
made important data available, I am particularly indebted to the
following persons:

In Denmark: Peder Hedebol, Minister of Finance; Director
H.Hj. Johansen of the Copenhagen Municipal Housing Depart-
ment and his assistant, Fuldmagtig C. Fulsang; Nils Fredricksen,
Director of the Danish Small Farm Holding Bureau; Peter Man-
niche, Principal of the International People's College at Elsinore;
Dr. Jorgen Pedersen, University of Arrhus; Viggo Holst-Knudsen,
Solicitor for the Copenhagen General Housing Society; Enrico
Hansen and Miss Edith Pihlglad of the Workmen's Co-operative
Housing Society; Tormod Jorgensen, retired Head of the School
for Small Holders at Høng; R. Rasmussen, Architect for Small
Holdings; and Willie Brodenhoff of the Danish Foreign Office.

In Sweden: Albert Lilienberg, Chief of Town Planning, Stockholm; L. A. Dahlberg, Director of Stockholm Municipal Real Estate Office and his assistant, Pontus Cronstrand; Sigurd Westholm,

City Architect of Stockholm and his assistant, Pehr Danielsson; Nils Collin, Director of Swedish Colonization Bureau; V. Ekerot, Head of Sweden's Forest Subsistence Holdings Office; Evert Strokirk, Chief Engineer for Kooperativa Förbundet; and Carl Bergeustralile in the Ministry of Foreign Affairs.

In Finland: B. Brunila, Town Planning Architect for Helsinki; Dr. O. W. Willandt, Director, Research Bureau of the Pellervo Society of Finland; Pekka Railo, Secretary, Workers Educational Association; Miss Ragnhild Ahlgvist, Librarian for the Finnish Architectural Society; Mrs. Rabel Lyytinen of the Finnish Foreign Press Office; and Miss Nina Strandberg of the Finnish Travel Bureau.

In Norway: Harald Aars, City Architect for Oslo; S. Forberg, Secretary, Department of Agriculture; Jacob Vindes, Chief of the Press Bureau, Ministry of Foreign Affairs; and Johannes Hoie, Assistant Director of the Small Holders School at Hvam.

The Municipal Real Estate Office in Stockholm permitted quotations from official documents; a similar privilege was extended by the City of Copenhagen. Extracts were taken from articles appearing in the *International Observer,* edited by Peter Manniche. Quotation was made from the report of the International Labor Office, Geneva, entitled *Housing in Europe,* and in the United States from the report of the Great Plains Committee, *The Future of the Great Plains.* Erskine Caldwell was kind enough to permit quotation from a copyrighted article appearing in the magazine, *Rural America.*

Also I desire to record the courtesies extended to me by the Royal Institute of British Architects through the Assistant Secretary, C. D. Spragg. Finally, I wish to express my appreciation to Theodore Sibley, who read parts of the manuscript and made helpful suggestions in arrangement. Erik Tore Rahm, in Stockholm, translated material into English for the purposes of this study.

J. G., JR.

CONTENTS

LIST OF ILLUSTRATIONS

xvi

HOUSING IN SCANDINAVIA

1. LAND FOR HOUSING

"GIVE ME WHERE I MAY STAND AND I WILL MOVE the world," said Archimedes. He was referring to the principle of the lever. Today, after more than two thousand years, we can fittingly apply the same remark to our search for land for housing purposes in urban communities. If housing is the lever, land is the fulcrum.

Recently, a housing official from a middle western city said to me, "When we have built on our present three sites I don't know where we can get any more land at a dollar a square foot. Land in our congested slum areas, where new housing is acutely needed, is held at too high a figure. We are blocked."

This problem of land acquisition is widespread today. Our American cities, in their rapid growth, have been more concerned in land transactions with the profits accruing to individuals than with any consideration of community advantages. Speculation in land values and unrestrained exploitation have been responsible for the artificial and excessive land prices.

The Scandinavian countries were faced with this same problem of land exploitation, but in the last quarter of a century they have initiated and are now fostering a new land policy, both in the urban and rural areas. One of the main purposes of this policy is to provide land for housing and to make community planning effective. This land policy has contributed substantially toward the success of Scandinavian

3

housing. Before we can describe this housing, it is necessary to make clear something of the philosophy underlying the land policy.

Chesterton once said, "The man in Bedford is not conscious of Bedfordshire. Our urban population has virtually forgotten that we live on the land." Land is the base of all economic life and the source of all production. Therefore, in the quest for workable social structures, the land question must be given first consideration. We are just beginning to realize this fact.

Through the ages land has been considered as private property: a commodity to purchase, acquire by gift, seize, possess, control, hoard, exchange, or sell, and to use, exploit, or abuse at will. The expression, "This is my land, I can do what I want with it," is familiar and carries with it an authority which brooks no questioning or interference.

This attitude ignores the fact that in reality land value is dependent on the presence of people. A successful real estate man in one of our large cities wrote in his biography two decades ago, "Any fool can say that a particular piece of property will become valuable some day, but it is the astute man who can say *when* this will occur and be able to hold the property, paying the interest and taxes over the years, until the demand for it is such that he can sell for a profit." It takes the presence of people to bring about the demand which determines land value.

Since land value is created in this way and not by the expenditure of labor, obviously it is a contribution of the community and its value is a social one. On the other hand, buildings and other forms of improvement of the land brought about by the expenditure of labor and subject to destruction and replacement can be properly considered as capital value.*

---

* See George Raymond Geiger, *The Theory of the Land Question* (New York, Macmillan Company, 1936), pp. 18–102.

It is necessary, therefore, to make a sharp distinction between the social value of land and the capital value of the improvements placed on it. Unfortunately, in our economy the social value has been absorbed by capital value, to the detriment of both. To illustrate: Some five years ago an operative builder bought a vacant tract of land in the suburbs of a large city. It comprised about fifteen acres. An arterial highway carrying heavy traffic skirted one side. In the six years I had lived in the neighborhood this traffic had trebled, and the indications were that it would continue to increase in the same ratio. The operative builder, without recourse to technical skill and without aesthetic illusions, laid out subdividing streets in a monotonous pattern reminiscent of the Roman camp, not giving any consideration to the hazard of the highway.

He then built his houses in successive steps, the first ones facing the highway, the others retreating inward toward the rear property line like an army on the rout; after two years time, the ground was entirely covered. It was a cosmopolitan display, a meeting of architectural styles from all over the globe brought together to solve a local housing problem. English castles, Georgian mansions, Italian villas, Colonial farmhouses, and modern "fishbowls," all thrown together without any racial segregation. Of this stew one might catch the spirit of world friendliness, the lion lying down with the lamb and all the animals happy. But the vision of the operator was practical; he knew the frailties of his buying public. He had a different fly for each kind of fish. Exposed to the view of passing Sunday motorists the houses along the highway sold first: one, an English shooting lodge of doubtful ancestry; another, a Mount Vernon homestead enclosed by a low picket fence; and the third, a sort of Florentine palace with a red tile roof and blue front door. In spite of the fact that the purchase prices were high, the builder disposed of his houses within a reasonable time.

After a few years the seeds of blight sprouted; the first settlers along the highway, because of the ever increasing noise and dirt, sold out at a figure substantially lower than the price they had originally paid. These lower sale prices immediately affected the value of the whole development. The second line of houses removed from the highway became vulnerable; more dissatisfaction among owners occurred and more sales followed, always at a lowering figure. The menacing highway and the haphazard arrangement of site plan had unleashed the forces of economic disintegration. The law of diminishing return came into operation and would-be investors in homes for enjoyable living found themselves the victims of a speculative adventure in real estate with no court of redress to turn to. In the spirit of the Light Brigade, "Theirs not to reason why, theirs but to do and *buy*."

The moral here is obvious. Had this plot of vacant land been considered at the beginning in terms of social value and carefully planned for its best use to the community as a whole, whether for houses, business enterprises, or parks, in part or in whole, the investment losses to the individual buyers would not have occurred, nor would the surrounding values have suffered from the deflation of this section. By putting land in the same category with capital and joining it with a capital improvement, land, the victim, was made an improper accomplice in a speculative venture.

To declare that the social value of land should be recognized is not to indicate that it should be treated as communal property. This is a primitive conception, quite out of line with our national economy. Rather, it is to recognize that the community has the prior right in determining, both for the present and the future, the proper use of land, whether its use is to be for purposes of housing, manufacturing, commercial or agricultural use, forestry or public parks. By this recognition the benefits to the individual are actually increased, because, by

putting land to its best use, its value is protected and pre-
served.

It may thus be said that the proper mission of land is to
function as a catalytic agent, assisting capital to develop resources and ministering to individual and community needs,
but without in any way losing its identity as land or relin-
quishing any part of its inherent value. Therefore, in a social
conception of land value, what the individual owns is not the
actual land but the privilege of putting that land to its best use
as determined by society.

This concept of the social value of land is a far cry from the
idea that land is a commodity lending itself readily to speculation and exploitation for private gain and subject to the ca-
pricious fluctuations of capital; yet in Scandinavia we find that
land is taking on this social quality. Without destroying the
idea of private property, Scandinavians emphasize the social
value of land. Their extensive and farsighted land acquisition
policy is based on this general principle.

Over a period of years Copenhagen, Helsinki, and Stockholm, the respective capitals of Denmark, Finland, and Sweden, have been steadily acquiring parcels of land, principally
within and around their limits. Each year sees an increase in
the holdings. This policy is not in practice to any extent in
Oslo, Norway. In 1936, the municipality of Copenhagen owned
some eight thousand acres on the outskirts of the city and over
three thousand acres within the city. Helsinki owns almost
thirteen thousand acres in its suburbs. Stockholm has acquired
approximately twenty-one thousand acres.

The purpose behind this municipal land ownership program, as expressed by the Stockholm authorities, is "to secure
sites for housing purposes and to influence the price of land so
that unbridled speculation will be prevented." In viewing the
land purchase and lease policies of Copenhagen, the local officials describe the broad objectives as "those which will give

the city the opportunity after a long span of years to change the city plan, to obtain centrally located sites for municipal needs, and finally to permit easy and inexpensive access to those parts of the city which might have developed into slums."

Copenhagen has a long tradition in municipal land ownership. Records show that as far back as 1100 A.D., when Copenhagen took its first steps toward becoming *kobstad* (a large town), the unfenced fields belonging to the peasants came into public possession. Several hundred years later an adjoining village, ruined in a siege, was purchased outright by the city. All the land thus acquired was rented to individuals, not sold. The tradition was threatened in 1795 after the great fire of Copenhagen. There was need for restoration funds. The king, loathe to increase taxes, appointed a commission to determine the method of raising the money, and the commission recommended the sale of a part of the city-owned property. The government opposed this recommendation, setting forth its views in a remarkable statement that deserves to be historic: "The operation of partitioning out ground and selling it for private use may give an immediate advantage and is within the province of private business, but is not a suitable undertaking for public bodies which must always pay more attention to lasting advantages than to immediate ones. The property and ground of Copenhagen belong to the city and its inhabitants, those of the future no less than of the present; therefore, any attempt to take away from future generations the opportunity to utilize this property, to reap the benefits of increased usefulness is positively deplorable." * This statement gives the key to the philosophy of the social value of

---

* "Land Policies of the Municipality of Copenhagen," Municipal Document, Copenhagen, 1936. (Translated from the Danish for the purposes of this study.)

land. Its truth is as applicable today as when it was written.

Fortunately, the proposal to sell the city lands was disregarded by the Copenhagen government, and the property remained intact. After many decades a large part of it was gradually permitted to pass out of the hands of the city. By the close of the nineteenth century, Copenhagen owned comparatively little ground, and it was then that the city, under a Conservative government, embarked on its land purchase program, a practice which is being continued today. It is refreshing to note how this new policy was initiated: As it was stated to me, the Conservative party "turned its course from political considerations to social considerations." Land again took on social import.

In Copenhagen, I discussed the land buying policy with Mr. Peder Hedebol, Minister of Finance, who was in direct charge of this work. We sat in a spacious but modestly furnished office of the Town Hall. Mr. Hedebol spoke quite good English. "I know your country a little," he said. "I made a trip to the United States some years ago." When I asked about the Copenhagen policy, he replied, "The city started buying available land in the 1890's under a Conservative Minister of Finance, and we have continued the practice ever since. In some years we have bought more than in others, but regardless of the form of government, whether conservative or liberal, the policy has been maintained. As you know, the Social Democratic party is now in office and they put more stress on land purchase than would be the case if the Conservatives were in power. The main purpose of this policy is to plan for the future growth of the city. By gaining possession of the land now, we avoid future high land costs and speculation. We are thus able to control the future development of our city.

"Land for future use is bought principally in the environs of Copenhagen; some areas are quite far out." He turned to a map on the wall and pointed out the large areas that had been acquired over the years. "This land will be used for future schools, parks, playgrounds, and public buildings of various kinds, and, of great importance, we will have available sites for housing, both of a social and a private nature." I asked if any definite plan as to location was adhered to in the acquirement. "No," he answered, "not a definite plan, but we do more or less follow a general plan. We think that it is not possible to determine in advance in just what direction the city will grow. Therefore we follow two courses: we buy according to a general plan and also at random. We buy mainly in those sections made accessible by existing railroads or highways, and also purchase ground in areas where we feel land might be tapped by future transportation lines.

"We pay market prices. There is no expropriation. We are always on the lookout for property. If a farm or an estate comes on the market in an area that interests us, we immediately make an investigation of the location, condition of soil, asking price, and other features. If we can agree with the seller on a price, we then submit the offer to the proper land purchase board with our recommendation. After purchase, if we have no immediate use for the land, it is leased at a nominal rental. The lessee pays the taxes, but the total amount of his payment for rent is usually not sufficient to carry the land. However, we consider the advantages gained by the city in having land available for future social use outweighs the small cost of carrying it. To stimulate our purchases further we customarily advertise in the newspapers in the spring of the year, asking for offers of land and when they are received the same method of examination and purchase is carried out."

If one glances at the land purchase map of the country surrounding Copenhagen, the formation of a very definite pattern of land acquirement can be noted. A green belt, stretching from sea to sea and encompassing the city, is being formed. Like defense outposts, important suburban towns are being surrounded by public land as protective cover, giving control of a future plan. Towns and villages like Lyngby, Gladsakse, Herlev, Skovlunde, and Bröndbvester will one of these days be a part of Greater Copenhagen.

The city of Copenhagen has also been acquiring property within the city limits, but the practice is motivated more by immediate needs than future ones. The land is usually bought at market value, but the municipality has the right of condemnation and uses it on occasions. If the price cannot be agreed upon, an arbitrator is called in and his decision is final. In determining market value, consideration is given to the rent returns of the building or buildings in the vicinity. It often happens that older buildings, because of their greater land coverage or because of the fact that they were erected at a time when building costs were low, yield a higher rent return than the newer buildings. Therefore in making the awards in condemnation procedure the newer buildings are somewhat penalized. This is considered a fault in the method of valuation.

As has been previously stated, the city owns considerable land within its boundaries. The land which is not reserved for public use by the city on the town plan is sold to private purchasers. The selling price is determined by market value or a value established by taking the original purchase price and adding interest and carrying charges over the years. City-owned land sold for low cost housing purposes, either to the municipal housing authorities or co-operative societies, undergoes a 5 per cent to 10 per cent deduction in price, due to the intended social nature of its use.

At the turn of the century the city, in selling certain parcels of land lying within its limits, retained the right up to the year 1972 to repurchase this land at the original purchase price plus the value of the improvements. This was done to avoid the mistakes which resulted previously in complete loss of control. Later this requirement became general. Recently a stricter condition has been added whereby land can be repurchased by the city after the year 1972 at the original sale price without consideration of the value of any improvements placed thereon. This stipulation is based on the assumption that, because of the rapid technical changes taking place in buildings and their equipment, they will be obsolete and valueless in forty years.

In thinking of Copenhagen one cannot forget that it was the inspiration of the immortal Hans Christian Andersen, the city that transformed itself so readily into a wonderland for him, his Copenhagen. On a quaint pattern of canals, cobblestone streets, spires, and chimney tops he spun his lovely tales. His gossamer fancy touched the child-heart in many lands, his name became famous the world over. The Danes are not unmindful of their heritage. They wish to protect and preserve the life-giving qualities of their city. They are aware of the civic disfigurement and devastation that follows in the wake of uncontrolled commercial and industrial development, and they want to give intelligent direction to these forces. Their land acquisition policy is sound and farsighted. They are but carrying out the principles laid down in 1795, "The property and ground of Copenhagen belong to the city and its inhabitants, those of the future no less than of the present. . . ."

Helsinki in Finland is the most northern capital in the world. Known as "the White City of the North," it supports a population of some two hundred and eighty-five thousand persons and its metropolitan area includes many more thousands living in the adjacent suburbs.

Helsinki's land acquirement program is extensive; the land

for the most part has been acquired in the past twenty years. As a result, the city now owns beyond its boundaries nearly thirteen thousand acres, an area twice the size of the city proper. The stated purpose is "to enable the municipal authorities to realize the town planning scheme; to provide sufficient building sites for the growing population, and thus to control the future development in every direction."

The city is built on a peninsula surrounded by deep water and sheltered by a fringe of islands. The approach by boat is magnificent. As we turned a pink granite point of one of these islands, suddenly a panorama of "the White City" appeared. Church spires in slender modern shapes were pencilled against a crystal-clear sky. One felt the transformation from European styles to something quite new and fascinating. An elderly man, a retired English architect, standing beside me on the top deck muttered sourly, "I say, I don't think I'm going to like this architecture." The evening before in the smoking room, without any introduction he had abruptly pounced upon us with, "I say, you two look like Americans. Are you?" He was a queer chap, most inconsistent; at one moment defying centuries of British custom by actually going out of his way to speak to us first, and the next moment retreating from something new and strange. "Really," I replied (which to the Englishman can mean anything or nothing), "give the town a break; wait until you have seen more of it!" Two days later he departed, still dissatisfied. Finnish architecture was too "modern" for him. He quietly admitted to me that when the Lord made English Gothic He broke the mold. Nothing else meant anything to him.

The natural setting of Helsinki encourages an enhancement of beauty and livability. And the Finns, eager to preserve their capital asset, are making use of town planning skill. Saarinen made a comprehensive plan for Greater Helsinki in 1918, and Bertel Jung also contributed his genius.

The work has been further developed by the municipal Town Planning Bureau. The town plan comprises the city proper and the surrounding suburbs, embracing an area of over twenty-five thousand acres and accommodating a future population of some six hundred and fifty thousand persons. To provide for future expansion, the city has under consideration the incorporation of now distant communities.

Though basic, the plan is flexible in its subordinate features. The authorities have expressed it well when they said, "The plan is used as a basis for the discussion of important questions; it does not claim to solve all problems in detail but it furnishes a point of departure."

Since we are concerned in housing with the facilities offered for recreation it is of interest to note that the plan sets aside for parks and playgrounds within the city boundaries an area in size equal to 26 per cent of the total area of the city. In addition, Helsinki has utilized its extensive water front and adjacent small islands for municipal bathing beaches and parks. In the plan for Greater Helsinki, with a future population of six hundred and fifty thousand persons, provision has been made for one acre of park for every 116 persons. Helsinki, by concerning itself primarily with better living conditions for its inhabitants, giving them open space to invigorate their bodies and beauty to refresh their minds, is building a city which at the same time appeals to visitors.

Again, in Helsinki it is vividly demonstrated that the proper functioning of a town plan depends basically on a sane solution of the land question. The practice of land purchase by the city proceeds at an average rate of some eight hundred acres a year. The amount varies year by year depending on the need, the availability of land, the funds at hand, and other factors involved. The method of acquisition follows closely that of Copenhagen; i.e., the land is bought in outlying sections at market value and is not acquired by expropriation. Portions of this land not needed for immediate or future public use in accordance with the town plan or other municipal purposes is leased to private individuals or public organizations. Today the annual lease rate is one Finnish mark a square meter, equivalent to a little less than two cents a square yard. The lease runs for a fifty-year period, with the stipulation that the city reserves the right at the end of every ten years to make adjustment in the rate. Rates vary somewhat in certain sections due to local conditions. The city contemplates, at the end of the first ten-year period, making a maximum increase of 15 per cent in the land rent, the exact amount dependent on location. Land owned by the municipality in the central parts of the city is usually sold outright.

In the garden suburb of Kottby, within the city limits, the municipality owns all the land. In 1920 a part of this land was leased by the municipality at the extremely low rate of one penni a square meter. In our measure this would be equivalent to leasing a lot twenty-five feet by a hundred feet for about twelve cents a year. The present rate for a plot of ground this size is about $5.50 a year. Is it any wonder that land costs are not a deterrent factor in construction projects, particularly as they relate to housing of either a private or a social nature!

As the city now owns large areas of land outside its limits and leases it at a fixed rate to all comers, there is little chance for land to acquire speculative significance and soar to high figures. On the other hand, as the city grows and the general scale of values increases, land value rises proportionately. Values in Helsinki are slowly increasing now. This may be considered a normal movement and quite different from the abrupt rise that springs from speculative activity.

Except for the colonization law (Lex Kallio) which applies to rural areas, expropriation of property is limited to land which will be used for streets, parks, and the like. It is not ap-

plicable to land for housing purposes. Perhaps the best reason why expropriation of property for housing in urban areas
is not legal is because there has been little need for it. The
city owns much available land, a condition brought about by
its wise acquisition policy over the years.

A tour in the outskirts of Helsinki shows the practical benefit of the policy. Kottby, to the northeast, is now one of the
older sections. It has been built up in parts with large and
small residences and provides a healthful environment for its
population. Newer sections like Gumtäckt and Masstad, laid
out by and under the control of the city, are now undergoing
development.

I had the pleasure of being shown over the city and suburbs by Architect B. Brunila, Director of the Municipal Town
Planning Bureau of Helsinki. (In Scandinavia there is a nice
custom of substituting the professional prefix "Architect" or
"Engineer" for our conventional "Mr.") He was an alert, en-
ergetic man, eager to furnish me with all the technical data
at his command, and in the English language, fortunately. I
mention this because I soon discovered that the Finnish language could not be trifled with. To understand or to speak it
takes special anatomical equipment found only in Finland.
Nature endowed these sturdy northern people with a heavy-
duty set of vocal cords and a well-lubricated tongue. Otherwise there could be no possibility of two Finns engaging in a
conversation! For instance, if you want to give the cheerful
salutation, "good morning," you say, *"hyvää päivää."* Confronted by this impediment it is easier and probably better to
refrain from speaking out at all. Again, suppose you want to
sit in the smoking car on a railway journey, you must ask for
the *"tupakoitsijoille."* One would feel ridiculous asking such
a question; better to give up entirely the thought of smoking
on the trip and sit in a nonsmoking compartment. But this
brings greater complications: to ask for a nonsmoking com-

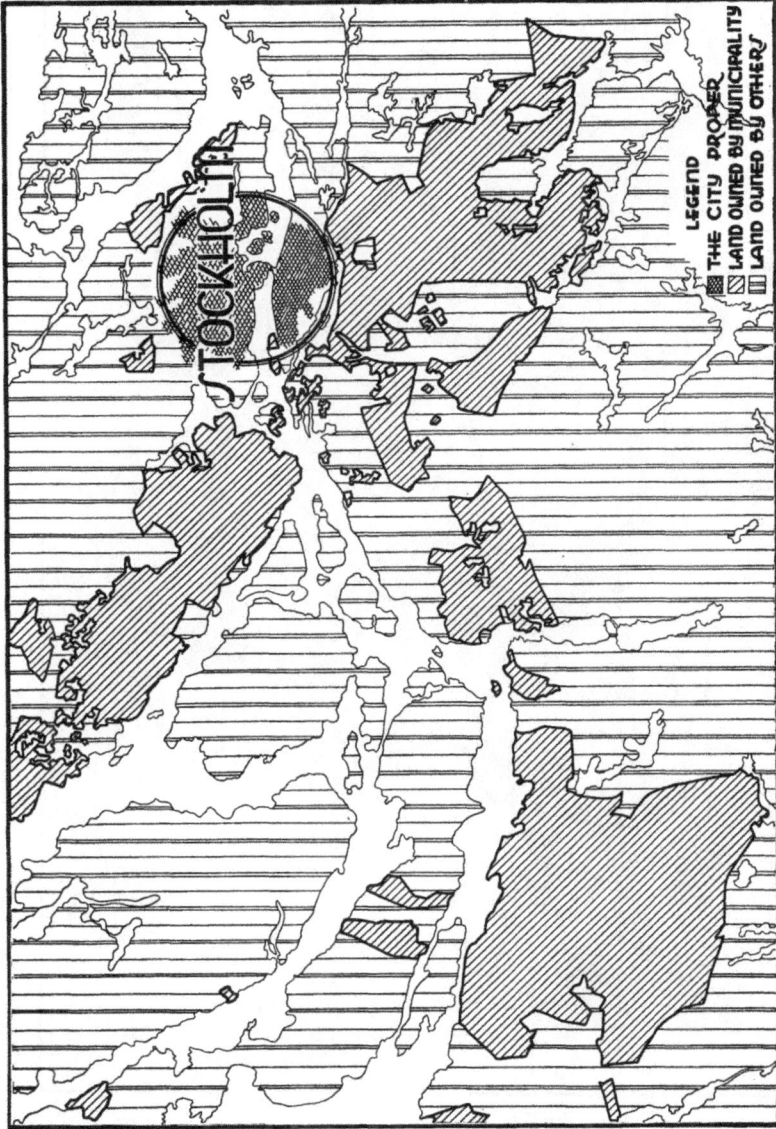

LEGEND

THE CITY PROPER
LAND OWNED BY MUNICIPALITY
LAND OWNED BY OTHERS

The land acquired by the city of Stockholm is to be developed as needed

LEGEND
THE CITY PROPER
LAND OWNED BY MUNICIPALITY
LAND OWNED BY OTHERS

The land acquired by the city of Copenhagen is held in reserve for future use

partment you must say *"tupakoitsemattomille."* This is out of
the question. Because of the language difficulty you are now
faced with abandonment of the trip altogether unless—and
the happy thought strikes you—unless they will let you ride
in the engine cab. The Finns being an accommodating people,
this probably could be arranged.

But to return to our tour, a stop was made to see the newly
completed wing of the municipal hospital. I gained the impression it was in full operation. We entered the basement
equipped for massage treatments and various kinds of baths,
all very modern and elaborate. (The Finns delight in cleanliness; perhaps it has a bearing on their honesty!) We walked
to the first floor, visiting wards and rooms containing special
equipment. We then took a self-operating elevator to the roof
and stepped out on a sun deck where a long line of white cots
were tucked in under a glass enclosed lean-to. In all our wan-
derings through this hospital, up to this moment we had not
seen a single patient, nurse, or doctor. The stage was perfectly
set but the actors were missing. I turned to Architect Brunila
and slyly remarked, "It's all very impressive, but where are
the patients?" He looked concerned and replied, "Wait, I will
show you." On our way down, we stopped at an intermedi-
ate floor, devoted entirely to wards. In the far corner of one
of these rooms we spied a wizened old chap in a dressing
gown sitting dejectedly on the edge of a bed, rubbing his
knee. Architect Brunila's face lightened; he touched my arm
and exclaimed triumphantly, "There is the patient!" *

Finland seems to have a great number of hospitals with very
few patients. One can hardly attribute this condition to excessive hospitalization costs. A young English chap in Helsinki
informed me that his two-week stay in the municipal hospital

---

* This incident has been thrown into tragic relief by the savage invasion of
Finland. The hospital, if it stands at all, is now probably filled with the inno-
cent victims of Russian bombings.

with an ignominious attack of measles was superior in comfort to a stay in any hotel. For board with excellent food and all services he was charged at a rate of about ninety-five cents a day. He said he was sorry he had been discharged! So, even taking into account a lower general scale of living costs in Finland than elsewhere, a reasonable amount of hospitalization would not make pulpwood of the family pocketbook.

Among the amenities of living for the people of Helsinki, mention must be made of the large municipal bathing beach within the city limits. Because of the comparatively short summer and their love of the out-of-doors, these people of the north feel that it is imperative to take full advantage of the sun's rays. To make the beach, sand was dredged from the channel and modern bathhouses were erected. The charge for use of a bathhouse is one mark or about two and a third cents in our money. Outdoor bathing for the people is not a luxury. It is within the reach of the poorer folk. Sings the immortal Kalevala:

> "To the shore I went to wash me,
> To the lake I went to bathe me."

In the manner of the old Swedish saying, "The flying bird gets something, the sitting bird nothing," Stockholm has not waited for housing problems to accumulate on her doorstep, but has advanced to meet them by initiating a progressive land policy and an equally forward-looking town planning program. Land acquisition by the municipality follows the general principles and practice of Copenhagen and Helsinki, but it is more extensive. The program is directly responsible for the development of the many attractive garden suburbs of Stockholm.

In the 1870's Swedish authorities began to show concern for the housing needs of the people. Industrialization had al-

ready started to attract workers to the urban centers. Shelter
was becoming scarce with an attending overcrowding. As a
result of this developing problem the city commenced about
1880 its purchases of land in the Inner City (Old City) of
Stockholm. The two-fold aim was to widen and relocate
streets in accordance with the early city plan and to provide
sites for housing. Land thus purchased and not used for
streets was sold to private individuals, who, for the most part,
built houses thereon. It was about this same period that the
suburban movement had its beginnings. Land purchase in the
Inner City continues today, and the money for this purpose
is taken out of the so-called street regulation land fund.

Also beginning in the eighties of the last century was a
movement toward the suburban areas of Stockholm. Private
enterprise was responsible for the development of the first
suburban communities of Djursholm and Saltsjöbaden. Since
that time, town plans and building regulations have, in the
main, directed the layout of suburbs.

Around the beginning of the century Stockholm experienced an acute housing shortage among the low income
groups. It was difficult to find cheap land on which workers
could build inexpensive homes. The city owned scarcely any
ground outside of its municipal boundaries. The situation was
desperate: the land problem brought about an impasse. Some
solution had to be found, and an investigating committee was
detailed to provide an answer.

Some years ago I asked a friend who had visited Scandinavia what he thought of the Swedes. He replied, "They are
a very practical people." The Swedes are practical in the
sense that if an idea appears sound to them by the test of
hard thinking, they waste no time in putting it into practice.

The committee came to the conclusion that the most effective way to bring about more housing at low cost would be
for the city to purchase, own, and control land in the subur-

ban areas of the city. As a result, Stockholm launched its land acquisition program in 1904, and this step was the turning point in the city's housing history. The first land acquired was located outside the existing city limits and consisted for the most part of large country estates. The land buying has continued over the years and today the municipality owns some twenty-one thousand acres within a distance of from two and a half to eight and a half miles from the center of the city. This area, about five times the size of the city proper, now contains garden suburbs to the south in the parishes of Enskede, Huddinge, and Brännkyrka, and to the west of Bromma and Spånga.

In 1907 the first comprehensive plan for the city was adopted and in this was incorporated the development plans for the garden suburbs in the Enskede and Bromma sections. Expanded city plans have directed the development of additional areas of city-owned land, turning them into picturesque garden suburbs which in an ever increasing way add to the beauty and livability of Stockholm.

The authorities regard the program thus: "From the beginning of the century, the city authorities have conscientiously endeavored to provide cheap building lots by municipal purchase and improvement of real estate. By so doing the city officials have been successful in preventing excessive land prices. . . . Furthermore, they have also been successful in directing the building of houses in suitable locations."

The land, after it has been laid out in lots in community developments by the city, is leased to private individuals. It is interesting to note, as officially stated, that up to the present the rent received by the city from its improved land more than covers the original cost of the land plus all development charges made by the city. In other words, the program has been "good business." American cities might well note this Swedish experience.

The lease period for the land is sixty years with the privilege of renewal. The occupant pays an annual ground rent amounting to 5 per cent of its value, said value being based on the purchase price of the land plus the cost to the city for the laying out of streets and installation of utilities. For a one-family-house lot the average rent is about ten cents a square yard, or for a lot twenty-five feet by one hundred and fifty feet, the ground rent would be in the neighborhood of $42 a year.

When a building is erected on a lot it may be encumbered by a mortgage in the customary manner. In the case of the sale of a house, the purchaser pays the agreed price to the owner and at the same time assumes the land rent of the city. This land rent system applies to ground in the suburbs (or Outer City) of Stockholm. In the Inner City, property owned by the city is sold to private enterprise at prevailing market prices. The city may also sell its land in the Inner City area at a figure lower than the market value when the city is assured that the land will be put to a social use, or, as expressed by the Stockholm authorities, "when the city is certain that the benefit of the low price of the land will actually redound to the good of the tenants and not to the advantage of the purchaser."

The main purpose of the city in this land purchase program was, from the beginning, to cater to the housing needs of persons without sufficient capital to provide homes for themselves. But in the course of time the inevitable happened: between the years 1920 and 1927, families of higher income flocked to the cheap land and built their homes. As a consequence, the municipal government decided to intervene and as an experiment built in the spring of 1927 some two hundred workmen's cottages composed of four rooms and basement. Out of this experiment developed the "Self-Help Plan," a unique and successful housing scheme.

Municipal land acquisition and town planning go hand in hand. Their marriage is necessary; there can be no single blessedness for either.

The old Urban Building Act of 1874 of Sweden was superseded by a Town Planning Act of 1907. Under the Urban Building Act the preparation of plans for towns and communities was authorized but was found to be meaningless "as such plans got no further than paper because in carrying them into effect the community had not the support of law, and was dependent on the faith and goodwill of private landowners. This impossible state of affairs was abolished by the Town Planning Act." * The legislation of 1907 was the first town planning measure of a modern nature introduced in Sweden. It stressed the importance of a town planning policy and, as expressed by the Swedes, "it established a judicial relationship between the municipality and the individual." It was not however, until the Town Planning Act of 1931 was passed that building regulations were promulgated and the principle of adherence to an approved town plan for cities and urban districts was made mandatory. Today, town plans have been prepared and are functioning in over four hundred and fifty urban communities in Sweden.

It is not the purpose here to state in detail the provisions of the 1931 act. Such a task would too severely tax the patience of the reader. On the other hand it is not well to sink to the depths of brevity as suggested by Mark Twain in one of his travel sketches. He remarked that in dealing with a string of intricate facts he often wrote, "The details of this tremendous episode are all too familiar to the reader to need repeating here." He said it sounded impressive and saved him the work of posting himself. We will, therefore, take the middle

---

* "Housing of the City of Stockholm," Municipal Real Estate Office paper, Stockholm, 1936. (Translated from the Swedish.)

course in describing a few of the important features of the law.

Throughout Sweden town planning for urban communities is under the jurisdiction of local boards appointed by the local authorities. For a particular urban community the city architect and engineers prepare the plan under the direction of the board. Where no such officers exist, technicians are temporarily appointed for the purpose. The proposed plan is submitted to the public for criticism and comment. The final plan as approved by the board is presented to the municipal council. When approved, it is then sent to the state board and, if sanctioned by the government, it becomes legally effective. All building construction must conform to the town plan. The provincial governors have the power to allow minor changes.

The municipality has the right of expropriation of land designated for streets, parks, and for other public use. Expropriation may be specially authorized in cases where a plot of ground in a building block, needed for the best development of the town, cannot be acquired on reasonable terms. In carrying out street improvements, the abutting land can be expropriated by the municipality if the owner refuses to pay for the increased value of his property due to said improvement. In addition compulsory acquisition of land is permitted: first, for housing purposes in built-up areas at railway stations, harbors, fishing ports, or other densely populated places; and second, to erect buildings for purposes of public discussion, religious enlightment, education, and the advancement of temperance.

In expropriation procedure, when the value of the land cannot be agreed upon by the municipality and the private owner, the case goes to a board of arbitrators. Five persons constitute the board: two from the municipality, two representing the owner, and a neutral person who presides as chairman. A panel of neutral persons of reputation and integrity is periodically appointed by the king, and the chairmen are drawn from this panel.

When building construction in the already improved areas has reached an advanced point, municipalities must extend the existing streets. In other words, there must be improved ground available to builders. The municipality must purchase the land of a private owner if the town plan designates that that land be reserved for public use. If a city plan is in preparation, the municipality can prohibit building construction in any area or areas for the period of a year.

When a town plan embraces private land which at some future time will be developed into building sites for sale, the owner must deed over to the municipality for streets, parks, sites for schools, etc., at least 40 per cent of the total area of the land, and when street improvements are made within the area, the owner must compensate the city for the costs. In initiating the development of private property, the developer must go to the town planning office for a site plan or for approval if one is privately made.

The practice of zoning, whereby urban areas are divided into sections and designated as to kinds of building and types of construction, is not employed in Stockholm. The town plan usurps this function. It designates the location of streets, building lots, markets, parks, playgrounds, traffic and transportation areas, cemeteries, athletic fields, water areas, and the like, and it establishes regulations for each city block. It specifies the maximum height for each building to be erected in the block and, if an apartment house, the number of apartments allowed. It declares the maximum width of buildings and the open spaces between them; the ground to be built on or left open. Also, it specifies the kind of building which may be erected, whether it shall be for commercial, industrial, housing, or public use. In this way each block becomes a planned unit in a general scheme.

It is recognized that because economic and social trends cannot always be anticipated correctly the plan should have elasticity and be subject to change. Therefore it has been found feasible to prepare only a skeleton plan for sparsely populated outlying sections where there is little or no sign of early development. These skeleton plans usually designate the main streets, give the height and extent of future buildings and the uses to which the area can be put. In general, only two-story houses can be erected in these areas, and the lots must not be less than about a quarter of an acre in size. In a sense, these skeleton plans are similar to zoning.

It has been found that the town plans submitted to the central government for approval vary in merit. The inferior character of some can be attributed to a lack of familiarity with town planning procedure and inadequate statistical data in the less advanced communities. Also, there appears to be a shortage of experts in the field of town planning. It is expected that time and education will correct these deficiencies.

Stockholm is built on thirteen islands; consequently one is pleasingly refreshed by views across water. Vistas between buildings terminate in miniature seascapes; streets lead to bay fronts unmarred by ugly structures. Not all vistas, not all streets, but the many opportunities afforded do readily give this lasting impression. To shift one's tired eyes from swirling, agitated traffic to the placidity of water is a blessed relief. To be able to turn one's back on masses of hurrying people and gaze across not far distant islands where details are lost in the splendor of mass effects is restful. It almost seems that the presence of water, whether it be in the form of natural bays or of artificial lakes is required by the modern city in a modern age. Stockholm is indeed fortunate.

It is not surprising that the town fathers decided to place their magnificent Town Hall at the water's edge. As a masterpiece of architecture its praises have already been widely sung.

However, to see a beautiful building at the sunset hour from the vantage point of a high terrace is bound to provoke expression. It was five o'clock in the afternoon and beneath me in the immediate foreground hurried a spent humanity. The city had issued a nightly parole to its toilers. Office workers, factory workers, shoppers, a medley of people in crowded tram cars and busses, in motor cars, in trucks, on bicycles, and on foot streamed by. Over the heads of this cavalcade, a quarter of a mile away, silhouetted against the magenta stained clouds of a western sky stood the graceful form of the Town Hall. In a few moments the dipping sun slipped loose from its vaporous cover and with corona effect slowly sank down behind the tower of the Town Hall.

The office of the Director of Town Planning is appropriately placed in the Town Hall building. I had an appointment with the distinguished director, Mr. Albert Lilienberg, but without the services of a guide I experienced difficulty in finding his office. After a very circuitous ramble which took me through some remote corners of this building, I found myself at the end of a corridor and in front of an imposing door. A neat brass plate bore in Swedish an official title which I, in all innocence, assumed to be that of "Town Planner." I boldly knocked. A resonate voice uttered some strange sound which I interpreted to mean "Come in." My first efforts to open the door were not successful—something was sticking. I tried again, applying pressure—still more pressure—the weight of my body was now in play, shoulder against panel, both hands turning the knob. There was a moment of extreme exertion. Suddenly the door swung inward and I was pitched headlong onto an expanse of rug in the middle of a large room. Pulling myself together I beheld a middle-aged man seated behind a large walnut desk. He looked quite startled. I made a brief apology for my awkward entrance and started to explain my mission. He slowly rose from his seat and then silently walked out of the room. "Rather a frigid welcome," I thought. In a few moments he returned followed by a tallish man with a high, glistening pink forehead and a bald head. This chap informed me that his chief did not speak English, but that he would attempt to help me. I explained that I had started out on an expedition to find the office of Director Lilienberg and had fallen by the way. "Oh," he said, "that is not difficult. It is at the far end of the corridor on the floor above. I will show you."

Mr. Lilienberg received me warmly. I wished particularly to get his views on the land acquisition policy as he had for many year seen the program in operation and had helped to direct its course. He stated that, in the first place, the operation of land purchase in the suburban sections had completely removed the speculative element and consequently there had been no rise in land prices. The idea of garden suburbs came over from England, and he mentioned Ebenezer Howard's book, *Tomorrow* * as playing an influential part in the adoption of the principle in Stockholm. He also told me that the governing system of leasehold in Stockholm was not in operation to any extent in other Swedish cities.

Mentioning some of the far-reaching benefits of the city's purchase of land and its controlled development under the Town Planning Act, he said, "As you know, the law states that when a private owner of a tract of land in the suburbs wishes to subdivide the land into building lots, he must not only secure the government's approval of his site plan, but donate a minimum of 40 per cent of the area of the tract to the city for streets, playgrounds, parks, etc. Now, when the city makes a development of its own land, it reserves as much as from 40 to 60 per cent of the area for these purposes, thereby setting a higher standard than is legally required. Therefore the pri-

---

* Sir Ebenezer Howard, *Tomorrow, a Peaceful Path to Real Reform* (Sonnenschein and Co., Ltd., London, 1902).

vate owner, in order to have his development appear equally desirable, finds it expedient to devote more than the required 40 per cent to streets and open space. In other words, the city establishes a standard and the public is the beneficiary."

I can hear a reader indignantly exclaim, "The city is going into the real estate business, and the private landowner is unjustly penalized." The answer is that it all depends on where the emphasis is placed. If we hearken to the Scandinavian way—and again I quote the principle laid down by the Danes in 1795, "The property and ground of the city of Copenhagen belong to the city and its inhabitants, those of the future no less than of the present. . . ."—we put the emphasis on permanent benefits to the community as a whole rather than on illusory satisfaction to the individual.

In a certain large eastern city a prominent real estate operator proudly announced his ambition: "I want to leave a million dollars apiece to my children." He had set for himself a sizable task because his children were exceedingly numerous. Under his commercial-minded and clever generalship, gaudy unplanned communities jammed with hundreds of tinsel-bedecked houses began shooting up like mushrooms in damp shade. In 1929 his operations were running full blast. Then came the depressed period of the thirties when "Brer Rabbit, he lay low." More fortunate than many of his fellow operators, he ran through the business storm keeping a part of his shirt and his giddy ambition. Today he is back at his old stand, littering up the countryside with more flimsy tinderboxes and it looks as though the children will get their legacy. But who benefits? The father satisfies an exaggerated vanity, dies early from strain, and receives the equivalent of a state funeral. The children are provided with enough leisure to engage in fratricidal struggle over their inheritance for the rest of their days and the mushroom communities become a blot on the landscape and an irretrievable loss in property value to the unfortunate homeowners. No one is benefited and the future of all concerned has been jeopardized.

Land exploitation in the United States has taken on the characteristics of a social menace and now threatens the life line of construction in low cost housing. In Scandinavia an intelligent answer to the land question has been found. It lies in a policy which should command the attention of all who are concerned with the problem of low cost housing.

2. MUNICIPAL HOUSING

MUNICIPAL SUBSIDY FOR HOUSING EXISTED IN Scandinavia before 1900, but it was only sporadically applied. Prior to this time, legislative acts were chiefly concerned with preventing and correcting unhygienic and unsafe housing conditions. It was the shortage of dwellings for the low income groups during and after the World War which brought state financial aid into the housing field. A similar housing crisis prevailed in Europe at the time, largely caused by the influx of workers from rural areas to industrial urban centers.

Private industry had not been able to meet the housing need. It could not provide dwellings for the low income group at rents that they could afford to pay. Landlords objected to lowering high rents because they believed it would endanger their invested capital. As stated in a Danish report, "It was feared that many landlords would turn the situation to their own advantage by making the most out of their tenants." *

Copenhagen, faced with the housing shortage of the war period, took drastic steps to relieve the condition. First it established restrictions on rent increases and then embarked with government aid on both a public and a private building program. Stockholm, Oslo, and Helsinki experienced a similar housing crisis and their respective governments also were compelled to intervene in such various ways as employing

---

* "Measures Taken by the Municipality of Copenhagen," Municipal Document, 1936.

rent restriction acts, extending state credit, and granting subsidies. In Oslo the municipality provided over 5,878 dwelling
units of various types; and in the five largest towns of Norway local authorities erected within a comparatively short period over half the total number of dwellings constructed.

In Sweden, to alleviate the hardships caused by rising rents,
a rent restriction act, passed in the spring of 1917, gave local
rent committees the power to establish rents and to exercise
control over evictions. These committees could also restrain
landlords from tearing down dwellings, joining them, or using
them for other than housing purposes. Considered from the
first a temporary measure to relieve the housing shortage, the
act was repealed in 1923.

State intervention started shortly before rent restrictions.
Between the years of 1916 and 1924 the city of Stockholm constructed some thirty-six hundred dwelling units, more than
half of which were of a temporary nature. At the same time
the state made outright grants of as much as a third of the
construction costs to builders. The intention was to make the
grant cover the amount of depreciation in value which was
expected at a later date when building costs would be at a
lower level. Continuing, in 1920 a State Housing Loan Fund
administered through the municipalities was established to
provide credit to builders. State subsidy to builders ceased
two years later, but loans out of the Housing Loan Fund were
granted up to and including 1930. Due to the depressed state
of the building industry occurring at this time, the government made further loans to builders through municipalities
with the main purpose of relieving unemployment. Upon re-
sumption of private building this policy was abandoned, and
as the latest expression of public intervention the state is now
engaged in extending credit to housing construction for low
income families with many children.

An important form of government intervention in the

Scandinavian countries has been the financial aid extended to the so-called public utility societies organized for the purpose of constructing housing. The term "public utility" is used to cover the various nonprofit or limited dividend organizations which, upon occasions, have been the recipients of government assistance in one form or another. The most common type is the co-operative housing society. The Scandinavian joint-stock housing societies, in which each member may become the owner of a number of dwelling units with the right to occupy, rent, or sell, cannot be classified as public utility.

It is interesting to note that in periods of critical housing shortages the municipalities have leaned heavily on public utility societies, supplying loans to them and in many cases owning the majority of shares of stock. And there are valid reasons why the governments of these countries have entrusted construction of housing to the public utility societies. Many municipalities, because of the necessary capital outlay for construction, found it financially easier and more efficient to extend credit to and use the facilities of the public utility societies than to engage directly in the work themselves. Also the public utility societies were often in a better position to manage the buildings erected.

Because of this situation, the municipalities in some of the countries have given greater emphasis to the public utility society than to municipal housing. This is true of the cities of Oslo and Helsinki, where virtually no municipal construction has been carried out within recent years. In the latter city this inaction has brought about a shortage of low rent housing and in consequence has caused serious overcrowding and hardship among the workers. In Copenhagen the present policy is to continue municipal construction of housing and at the same time to extend limited encouragement to the public utility societies.

In addition to the municipal and public utility housing

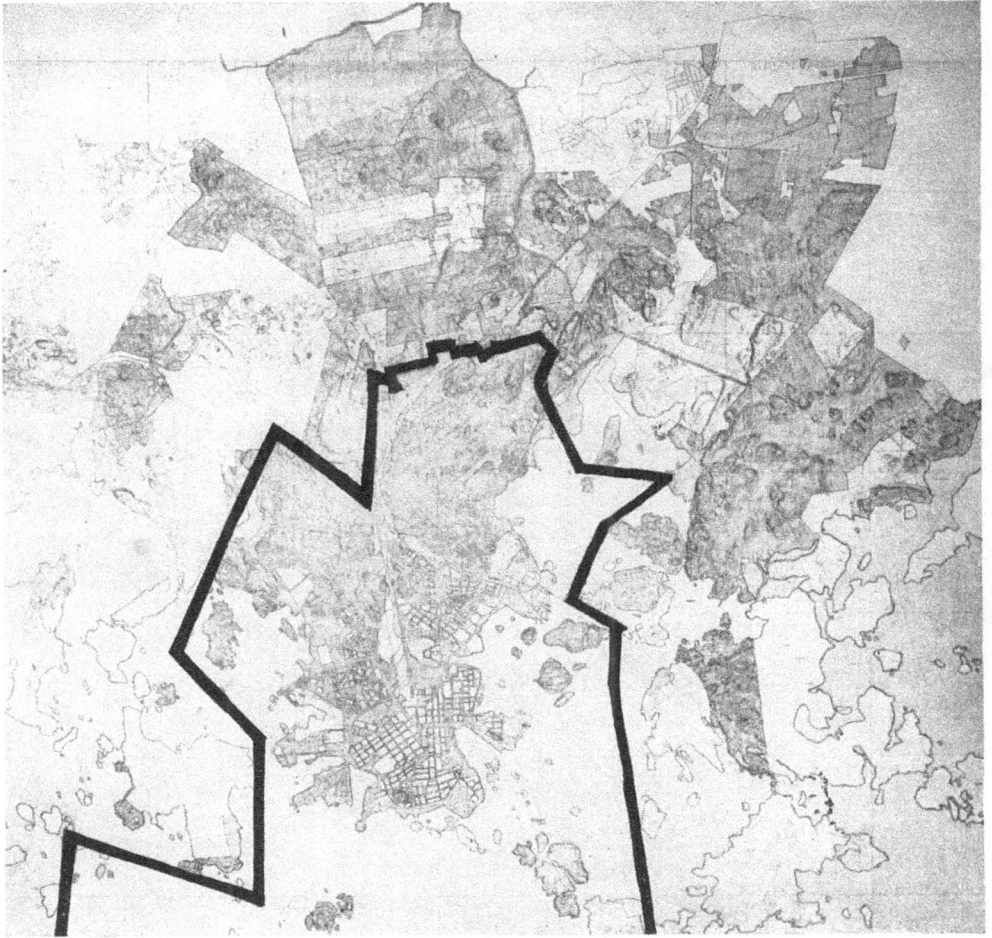

Map of HELSINKI

The city proper is shown within the black line. The shaded areas beyond indicate land owned by the city, most of it acquired in the last twenty years. The total is twice that of the city proper

COPENHAGEN

Panorama of municipal, co-operative, and private housing surrounding playground and large park

within the cities proper, we find a more open living offered by the well-planned garden suburbs of Stockholm and Helsinki. In Stockholm these garden suburbs are marked by a simple beauty and an unusual degree of orderliness. Here are found the small single homes with colorful exteriors, bordering on parks and playgrounds. Here live industrial workers, artisans, government employees, and others, all enjoying the amenities of a spacious environment.

As an additional consideration of the health and happiness of their citizens, the municipalities of Copenhagen, Helsinki, and Stockholm have taken a unique step in providing, within the city limits, so-called allotment gardens. These garden plots and miniature cottages are available to families of modest means and are used for summer living as an adjunct to the more confined apartment life. The cost of this form of municipal activity is small, but its value to society is substantial.

Copenhagen proper, including the municipalities of Frederiksberg and Gentofte, has a population of some eight hundred and thirty thousand persons, a city about the size of Baltimore.

Denmark has often been referred to as the country having reached the highest rung in the ladder of democracy. Equality is not talked about, it is practiced. Danish social legislation seems to indicate "something for all." In Copenhagen it is not difficult to discover symbols of this democratic spirit. For instance, the king has his name listed in the telephone book. Again, this same king rides horseback alone in the public parks and his subjects do not gape and stare, but carry on their own pursuits as though nothing unusual were happening. Even in the planning of new streets we glimpse this spirit of "something for all": You will observe a hard-surface roadbed for vehicle traffic; beside this and separated from it by a row of trees is a bridle trail of soft earth for horseback riders;

on beyond and slightly elevated is a path for bicyclers; and finally, there is the pavement for pedestrians. Drivers, riders, cyclists, pedestrians, all moving in their appointed course without confusion—a celestial order brought down to earth!

The same democratic idea has been applied to shelter. The municipality of Copenhagen has provided decent housing for the lowest income group, for those who are without sufficient means to secure accommodations for themselves. The wants of those with some available cash and a slightly higher income are satisfied by the co-operative societies. And lastly, private industry meets the requirements of those with more ample means. In the past, both the state and the municipality have aided all three types.

I sometimes wonder at the remarkable change that has taken place in less than a decade in the American public's attitude toward the slums of our large cities. Education and her handmaiden, publicity, have so effectively thrown the spotlight on the dark recesses of dirty back alleys, inside courts, and filth-laden hovels that cities now vie with one another in drawing attention to the extent and superiority of their slums. Only recently a visiting architect from Moscow declared in the press that an outstanding feature of New York was its many slums, the existence of which produced a terrific impression on him. New Yorkers were highly pleased because he had given them a triple-A rating in this field. Prior to this, another foreign visitor committed an indiscretion by only mildly condemning the Philadelphia slums. Instantly an indignant local slum patriot burst into print with the correction that "Philadelphia slums are the worst in the world." Then we hear of the superiority of Washington slums and Chicago slums with no equal. So it goes—American cities competing with each other in a mad race for slum supremacy!

I wanted to see the slums of Copenhagen, but I hesitated even to ask whether any existed for fear of insulting the immaculate city. But the authorities assured me that they were in existence. I was taken out to see them and I had reason to feel that they were typical and not put on view as were the "Villages of Potemkin." * I was disappointed; these slums were far too respectable-looking to be classified with the American product. Rooms were clean and tidy and flower pots stood on the window sills. The chief faults were that the dwellings were old and faced on small courts in the interior of blocks, and that central heat and modern sanitation were lacking.

While a certain amount of overcrowding exists in Copenhagen—a condition which spurs the authorities to provide new housing—it is less severe than in other cities of Europe. From available statistics it would seem that about 40 per cent of the population of European capitals occupy one-room dwellings, whereas in Copenhagen only about 7 per cent are in this category.

To relieve overcrowding and provide adequate housing for the lowest income group, the city of Copenhagen has erected since the year 1916, buildings containing over fifteen thousand apartment units and accommodating some fifty thousand persons. The cost to the municipality for this work has been approximately $26,000,000, and in addition the State of Denmark has advanced $2,225,000. In the years between 1931 and 1934 the municipality was particularly active in its construction of low rent housing, completing about twenty-one hundred apartment units.

In American procedure, the question has often arisen whether it is more desirable, under a given condition, to erect single houses or multiple dwellings, commonly known as apartment houses or flats. The municipality of Copenhagen in

---

* From the idiom, *"Potemkin' sche Dörfer,"* referring to the artful means taken by Potemkin, a Russian official, to dress up some wretched villages for a visit of Queen Catherine.

its early operations found that the dwelling unit costs of single cottages erected were some 30 per cent higher than the same unit costs in their four- and five-story apartment houses. Consequently, on the basis of cost alone further building of the single houses was abandoned and in recent years only multiple dwellings have been constructed. Danish authorities viewed the question in this way: "It is of importance to the municipality to build a great number of dwellings as cheaply as possible. Therefore it has principally erected apartment houses because dwelling units of this type are by far the most economical to construct." * Valid arguments sustain this point of view. Except in the older and more central parts of the city where the streets are narrow, Copenhagen gives the impression of spaciousness. Stretches of parks, playgrounds, watercourses, canals, wide streets, and comparatively low buildings contribute to this effect, and because of this, the municipal apartments in the form of large blocks do not produce the same feeling of congestion that would be found in many cities lacking these attributes.

When the Copenhagen authorities put the whole emphasis on providing housing accommodations for the greatest number of needy families, they are justified in their preference for the large, apartment type of building because of its lower unit dwelling cost. But when other important factors are taken into consideration, as they must be, the policy appears somewhat shortsighted. To construct only apartment buildings of four and five stories without elevators and central heat in an age of accelerated technical change, reflected in rising living requirements, is to invite premature obsolescence. And obsolete buildings, particularly those that house a great number of families, are much more likely to succumb to slum infection than are single houses of the same age. Therefore, this

---

* "Measures Taken by the Municipality of Copenhagen," Municipal Document, 1936.

policy of economy uninterruptedly pursued might lead to unsatisfactory consequences. As a supplement to the apartment house, one misses in Copenhagen the cottage type of municipal housing for the low income groups, which is found particularly in the suburbs of London and elsewhere. In these places even those of small income can gratify their craving for a more individual environment.

The lowest income families, workers in a variety of occupations, occupy the municipal apartments. It is mandatory for the city to provide living quarters for those unable to meet the rent demands of other housing, so admission to the municipal housing is based on the requirement that tenants be without sufficient funds, both initial cash and income, to secure accommodations in some of the workers' co-operative housing societies.

Four important factors have favored the municipality in providing housing for the low income groups in Copenhagen: (1) the availability of property previously secured by the municipality for social housing purposes; (2) the power to obtain additional land in central parts of the city by paying the current market value; (3) the availability of state and municipal loans at low rates of interest; and, finally, (4) the extension of government subsidy to poor families unable to meet rent levels.

In the past, at different times, several methods of finance have been used to further the construction of not only municipal housing but co-operative and private housing. Generally speaking, the financing has been done by subsidies from the state with and without municipal guarantees; by loans from the municipality; and by the municipality's guarantee of loans from private organizations. In addition, taxes on the property involved have been exempted upon occasions.

In the construction of municipal apartments, recent financial procedure has been along the following lines: A first mortgage up to 45 per cent of the total cost of the project is obtained from a mutual credit association and expires in a maximum period of sixty years, bearing interest as a rule at 4½ per cent; a second mortgage up to 55 per cent of the total cost of the building project is obtained from a second mortgage credit association and expires in forty years, bearing 4½ per cent interest; and a third mortgage from 55 per cent to 95 per cent of the cost is obtained from a savings bank or an insurance company, secured by a municipal guarantee of principal and interest. The remaining 5 per cent is advanced by the city.

Because of the moderate cost of both land and construction, rents in Copenhagen are substantially lower than in any of the other Scandinavian capitals; in certain sections they are only half as much as in Stockholm. Rents in the municipal apartments vary considerably, depending on costs at the time the buildings were constructed; they are lowest in those earliest built. More recently, municipal apartments are being taxed at the same rate as those privately constructed. The average rental for two rooms and kitchen (one room being a combination living-dining room and the other a sleeping alcove) is around $9.90 per month. In addition, gas for cooking costs from $1.15 to $1.38 per month. In terms of income, based on the housing census of 1930, the median rent in the city as a whole was shown to be as low as 15 per cent of a tenant's income.

COMPARISON OF RENTS IN THE SCANDINAVIAN CAPITALS

Average Annual Rent 1933–34	Stockholm	Copenhagen	Oslo	Helsinki
1 Room and Kitchen	$191	$ 68	$ 80	$160
2 Rooms and Kitchen	292	119	134	269
3 " " "	418	169	200	313
4 " " "	553	209	299	. . .

"To pluck *half* a plume from the wig of Shakespeare," it is curious the stuff recollections are made of. Commonplace scenes and trivial happenings do not always escape our perception. Some impressions fall asleep in our minds and then, months afterwards, awake with a start and, like a hungry child, cry for attention. If we wished to place the responsibility for an impression on its proper sense agent, we would no doubt say that sight was the greatest contributor. In many instances, however, taste and feeling predominate. For instance, we all know the tourist whose condemnation of a place has been based on a poorly cooked meal or a hard bed. To a very minor degree does the sense of smell create an impression. Only once do I recall hearing a returning traveller, after three days spent in the Eternal City on his first visit to Europe, declare with blushless candor, "Rome is one city I didn't like —too smelly!" But when we consider the sense of hearing we more often find that a particular sound, melodious or otherwise, produces a profound and lasting impression. For instance, my memory of a Sunday afternoon spent at Dorking, England, years ago is wholly associated with the glangorous outpourings of a legion of church bells furiously endeavouring to drown out the strident appeal of several Salvation Army bands operating on successive street corners. It was a riotous welcome to the newcomer and indelibly stamped itself on my mind. In this same realm of sound, two specific recollections of Copenhagen cling to me: one, the ever present and intimate tinkle of bicycle bells (every third person in Copenhagen not only owns a bicycle but exercises it daily), and the other, the noisy din of roller skates mixed with the merry laughter of children in the spacious courts of the municipal apartments.

The courts of these municipal apartments have undergone an evolutionary process. Air-mindedness, which transformed in shape the ancient automobile from a horseless carriage to the present streamlined form, has, in another way, been responsible for expanding the courts of the municipal buildings. The narrow enclosed court of apartment buildings erected before the World War was not designed to admit much air or light, but in the decade following, as the demand for air and light increased, courts expanded in size. The next development brought a further openness by building around only three sides of the court. The trend today is toward the use of the so-called lamel plan, which departs completely from the old block form and arranges buildings for the most part in parallel lines, separated from each other by landscaped courts.

As we entered the large inside court of a typical municipal apartment building, erected around 1930, a lively scene presented itself. Exuberant youngsters on roller skates were darting hither and thither over the pavement like agitated water-bugs; other children were skipping rope and playing games. When some of the older ones spied my movie camera, they made a rush in our direction to plead that their pictures be taken. Appeasement was necessary before we could proceed further. In examining housing projects in this country and abroad I have found that children delight in posing for the camera. But their mothers are more reticent. Rarely will they consent to the ordeal; either they feel they are not properly dressed or they distrust the motives of the photographer. It is as though the lens of the camera possessed the awful significance of an evil eye, making them as timid and apprehensive as wild animals at a water hole.

The court provided facilities both for recreation and for certain domestic operations of the housewives. Areas at the ends, along the sides, and in the middle of the court were hard-surfaced for children's play. The harshness of these areas was relieved by two fenced-in grass courts ornamented with trees and shrubs. Racks for drying clothes bordered the grass plots.

Two rows of sheds gave a sheltered play space in bad weather. One-story brick buildings, with ventilated eaves, housed garbage and refuse cans which were collected by the municipality three times a week. Finally, placed at strategic spots were several elevated racks for outdoor carpet beating, a very necessary convenience in maintaining the Danish tradition of cleanliness.

In appearance the building left much to be desired. Of five stories, its plain and somber gray brick walls gave it a decidedly institutional character. Its red tile roof, animated by a heterogeneous assortment of chimneys, bathroom ventilators, and attic vents completed the aesthetic devastation. From the practical side, knowing the fallibility of flashings around roof penetrations, I wondered how such a roof could be kept watertight. Like Peer Gynt, who, for every idol he sent to China also dispatched a missionary to allay his conscience, perhaps here under every ventilator a bucket is placed.

Because this building was of nonfireproof construction, the law required two means of egress from each apartment, i.e., two stairways: a main stair in fireproof enclosed walls and the other, a service stair of wood in ordinary frame walls. The service stair was not a pretentious affair, being snugly tucked in a space about the size of an ordinary closet. From the top floor it did not loiter on its way down—it nose-dived in swift, narrow spirals to the ground floor. Possibly a high mortality resulting from its use accounted for its abolition as a requirement in the present building laws! Now, in apartment houses of more than three stories only one fireproof stairway as an exit is required, provided each apartment unit has two small balconies. The idea is that in case a fire prevents the use of the main stairway, the balconies can become temporary ledges of safety for the occupants until the firemen arrive with their ladders. This might work if everyone remains orderly and calm on the balcony with no unnecessary shoving or crowd-

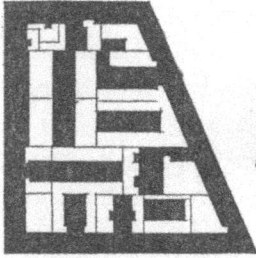

PERIOD 1860–1880   PERIOD AROUND 1900

AROUND 1912   AROUND 1928

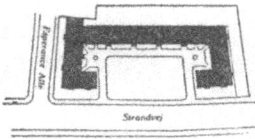

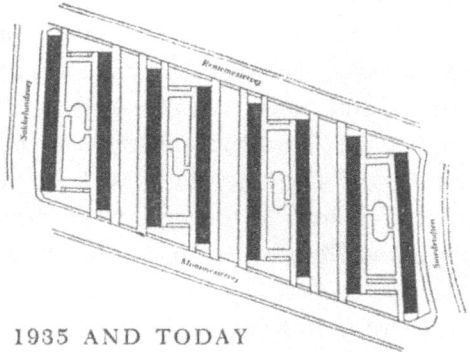

IN 1932   1935 AND TODAY

Evolution of the Plan of Apartment Houses
in Copenhagen

ing; if no attempts are made to jump before the firemen arrive; or if smoke is not pouring out of the window directly under the occupied balcony. But let us put such unpleasant possibilities out of our mind. Our principal mission was to see some of the individual apartments.

We ascended a stairway to the third floor and stopped in front of a door bearing a brightly polished brass name plate marked "M. Baumann." It was interesting to see a name plate. It gave a touch of dignified importance to the door and seemed to symbolize a recognition of the worth of ordinary citizenship in Denmark. Mrs. Baumann courteously welcomed us to her apartment. There were three rooms, a kitchen, and a handy yachtsman's bathroom which calls for a separate description. The parents and two children comprised the family. Mr. Baumann worked in a bakery. The rooms of their apartment were simply furnished and neat. The type of pictures on the walls surprised me. One did not encounter the cheap reproductions and sentimental prints customarily exemplified by the intrepid boy Daniel pacifying a collection of benign-looking lions, or that classical tear-gusher, "Breaking Home Ties." Instead, the walls were enlivened by original oil paintings of Danish landscapes. This preference for original oils and water colors I found to be quite common. 'Tis true, the pictures were not always what could be called the best art, but their quality reflected the cultural inclination of their owners. "My brother paints as a hobby," said Mrs. Baumann.

In one corner of the living room stood a large black stove garnished copiously with brass trimmings in the manner of the ancient and honorable T-Model Fords. This coal burner did double duty for the living room and the sleeping alcove adjoining. This was not unusual as most of the municipal apartments were heated entirely by room stoves. Only a few of the later buildings contained central heating plants, these having been provided more or less experimentally. The prevailing policy now is not to provide central heating plants for the municipal apartments, but to leave this more expensive equipment to co-operative and private housing.

The kitchen in the Baumann apartment was small but adequate. An early model sink stood under the window. The facilities for cooking were simple: two individual gas plates rested on a table top and were joined by hose connections to gas outlets at the rear wall. Ice refrigeration was lacking; instead, a "cooling" compartment, built into the kitchen dresser at the exterior wall-end and ventilated from outside, served the purpose. I was informed that this method was practical for the Danish climate and conditions—cool summers and daily supplies of fresh food. To the American housewife, geared up to flamboyant displays of "latest model" kitchen equipment in frequently promoted "home shows," this simple kitchen of a Danish municipal tenant might seem distressingly primitive. But it must be kept in mind that equipment, however simple, which actually functions within the dwelling unit in kitchen and bathroom is infinitely superior to the antiquated facilities found in the backyards and alleys of slums.

The compact bathroom of this apartment deserves more than a passing word. It treated lightly the traditional principles of bathroom planning, yet it seemed to perform its functions expeditiously and without shame. Its size, a little under three feet by five feet, gave it an air of intimate coziness. It actually started out in the world to be a shower stall and then found itself encumbered with a couple of dependents: a wash basin and a toilet. A shower head projected from the center of the ceiling and a drain in the tile floor caught the casual water from the shower that missed falling into the two receptacles. It was a one-man bathroom, the only limitation being that an occupant had to plan his activities in advance! A tiny vent in the ceiling made an insignificant gesture at ventilation. A small window opened into the service stairs. This bathroom left much to be desired, but again, it provided conveniences preferable to the outhouse in the back yard or a chilly bath taken in a washtub in the kitchen of a slum house.

We climbed a stairway to the attic. Here an intricate maze of ventilating pipes snaked their way to the roof, accounting for the multitudinous number of disfiguring vent openings we had previously observed outside. Partitioned compartments for the storage of goods of the different families were arranged along the sides.

No description of a municipal apartment building would be complete without some mention of that indispensable place in the basement where the Danish housewife does her weekly laundering. Here dirt met its Waterloo. There were separate rooms for the different operations. Hot water for the washing, heated by gas, was paid for on the meter system, the cost of a family wash being about twenty-five cents. There were ventilated drying rooms and curiously contrived hand-operated mangles, showing a blood relationship to the early printing press, which further aided the housewife. Other rooms in the basement contained racks for the family bicycles—the inexpensive Danish substitute for the automobile.

The basic materials used in construction of these municipal apartments are brick for the walls, wood for the interior, and tile for the roofs. Reinforced concrete has been employed only to a limited degree. Iron for building construction, even down to the very nails, has to be imported.

Local reports indicate that the construction cost of an apartment unit in Copenhagen is approximately $1,600, which is about one half the cost of a unit in Stockholm. There are several reasons for this: The cost of building materials and labor is less; because of a milder climate, thinner walls can be used; less money goes into heating equipment, and in general the buildings in Copenhagen are simpler in their arrangements and facilities. When a building cost index of 100 is taken for the year 1914, we find that costs reached a peak of 340 in 1920. After that costs gradually sank to a low of 150 in 1932. Recent years have brought a rise from this low point.

The municipal apartment buildings, containing over fifteen thousand dwelling units, provide accommodations for one twentieth of the total population of Copenhagen, and there are about one thousand shops and offices scattered through these buildings. The importance of this municipal activity, established in 1916, is shown in the size of the administration department. Today, a force of forty persons, headed by a director, assistant director, and chiefs of sites, demolitions, legal matters, and finance, comprise the office personnel. In addition there is a field force of over sixty persons. The plans are generally prepared by private architects.

While the Copenhagen authorities express satisfaction with the municipal housing accomplishments of the past they are aware of the need that still exists. Their view is expressed thusly: "Before it may be justly claimed that housing conditions are normal, a sufficient number of dwellings must be erected so that: (1) homeless people, now a charge on the municipality, are adequately provided for; (2) the existing overcrowding in flats is eliminated; (3) the inadequately housed persons in the summer homes of allotment gardens are taken care of; and finally, (4) there is a reserve of vacant, adequate housing." *

Speaking of statistics brings to my mind the old gentleman at the club, who, to introduce a pet story appropriately, would bang loudly on the table and then exclaim, "Speaking of noises, that reminds me . . ." and then he was off. Borrowing a similar excuse for digression, I would like to touch lightly

* "Measures Taken by the Municipality of Copenhagen," Municipal Document, 1936.

for a moment on the subject of collecting statistics. In my quest for housing data I encountered marked differences in the accessibility of records. For instance, there is no surface mining of Danish statistics. I knew they existed, but securing them was like tracking foxes over snowy ground and then laboriously digging them out of their holes. But the reward was usually worth the effort. I recall my second conference with a helpful Danish official who, after wrestling painfully for over an hour to give me his English version of some special Danish housing finance, abruptly mopped his moist brow and pleadingly inquired, "Can we stop now? I do not feel well. Will you come tomorrow, here?" I had several of these short but strenuous conferences with him and fortunately was able to obtain the desired facts without inducing his nervous collapse. Swedish statistics, on the contrary, are abundant and accessible, demonstrating in a nice way the businesslike mind of the Swede. However, without wishing to detract from the force of the compliment, experience compels me to offer an amendment. Perhaps Swedish statistics should remain in their mother tongue and not undergo the travail of translation into the English language. Something happens in the process: all sorts of meaningless words attach themselves to sentences like barnacles to a ship. I have before me at the moment a volume of translated records. It has all the luxuriant impenetrability of a Brazilian jungle. Cutting a way through the wordy vegetation has been no light task. So, to prevent the reader from becoming entangled in the statistical underbrush from which he might never escape, I will keep a reasonably tight rein on its presentation.

"There are, properly speaking, no slums in Stockholm as the word is understood in the United States," declares a Swedish report.* This can be accepted as true when we consider

* "City of Stockholm Housing," Document of Real Estate Office, Municipal Housing Department, Stockholm, 1936.

principally the disintegration of buildings and the wretched living conditions usually associated in our minds with American slums. If, however, we look upon the phase of overcrowding as an important factor the conditions in Sweden are by no means perfect. A 1933 housing census of fourteen Swedish towns showed that 50 per cent of the working-class families with three or more children under fifteen years of age were living in dwellings of one room and a kitchen. Also, in these same towns, 32 per cent of the living rooms in dwelling units were accommodating at least five persons for sleeping purposes. However, there has been a noticeable reduction of overcrowding in the past twenty years, due mainly to the smaller number of children in families of low income.

The lack of available accommodations at low rent has in reality imposed a penalty on the raising of large families and this condition has to a considerable extent been responsible for a decline in national birth rate. Disturbed by this decline, the authorities have recently instituted a program providing large families of slender means with suitable shelter at low rent.

As in many other countries, particularly England, the increase in the number of families in Sweden has been greater than the increase in population. Consequently, greater stress has been put on the production of small house units. In the towns and urban areas the trend has been in the main toward the displacement of the old burgher houses by apartment buildings, housing several families on a rent basis. Next in order numerically are privately owned homes, followed by apartments in co-operative dwellings, and institutional buildings. The last decade has shown an increase in the number of houses owned by occupant. In the past ten-year period 20 per cent of the building has been of a nonspeculative character; that is, it has been in co-operative and other public utility forms. It is expected that the trend in this direction will be

accelerated as more people discover that the construction profits ordinarily allocated to private promotion could be advantageously employed in the reduction of rents. As far as Stockholm is concerned, within the Inner City, apartment houses
of five and six stories predominate. In recent years, both in
the city proper and in the suburbs, apartment houses of three
and four stories, based on the lamel plan, have become popular. In the Outer City (suburban section), we find low-story
apartment buildings and single houses, the latter being the
most numerous and determining the character of the garden
suburbs.

A feminine admirer once exclaimed rapturously to James
McNeill Whistler, "I saw the Thames this morning and there
was an exquisite haze in the atmosphere which reminded me
so much of your paintings. Really, it was a perfect series of
Whistlers." "Yes, madam," replied Whistler gravely, "Nature
is creeping up." In a like manner, modern facilities are steadily
creeping into Swedish homes. There has been a marked increase in the installation of central heating plants, bathrooms,
interior water connections, and sewerage systems.

Much housing legislation has been ground out of the Swedish legislative mill. Like the tones of a radio, government intervention has blared forth loudly when needed and then
faded to a whisper as private enterprise, energized by the
stimulating measures, assumed the burden of building construction. During this ebb and flow of government assistance
certain beneficial and, for the most part, permanent provisions were incorporated in the system. Mention has already
been made of the farsighted land acquisition policy of Stockholm and the system of leasehold applying to the use of municipal land in the suburbs. As early as 1904 the government
established the Own Home Loan Fund from which persons
of slender means could borrow money for the construction
of dwellings. Another accomplishment was the establishing

of the City Mortgage Bank of the Kingdom of Sweden for the purpose of granting first mortgage loans, principally for the construction of apartment buildings. Two decades later, in 1929, the government set up a secondary credit agency known as the Swedish Housing Credit Bureau.

After the war, a frozen credit condition was thawed out by the creation of a State Housing Loan Fund, the purpose of which was to provide credit to building contractors. Again, to stimulate private building, in 1933 the Riksdag established a fund from which tertiary credit could be obtained up to 90 per cent of construction cost. In 1935 the Riksdag initiated its program to provide housing for large families of low income. And the latest chapter in the governmental intervention history has been the formation of a State Home-Furnishing Fund to aid engaged couples in furnishing their new homes. To summarize, government intervention in the housing field has been in the nature of: (1) grants and loans by the state; (2) grants and loans by the municipalities, and municipal guarantees of loans made by the state; (3) disposal of publically owned land at reduced prices, or gratis if the proposed building was to serve a social purpose; and, (4) low interest rates on government loans. Both the state and the municipalities have shared in advancing the housing program.

However, it must be noted that in comparison to other European countries the Swedish government has not been liberal in providing direct subsidy for housing purposes. It has preferred, rather, to assist mainly by the extension of cheap credit both to the co-operative societies and private industry. This cheap credit in the form of secondary and tertiary loans has accounted for over 20 per cent of the building construction carried on in the past quarter of a century. In recent years, chiefly for the relief of unemployment, considerable state funds have been available for construction and renovation in the rural areas.

The municipality of Stockholm owns and controls over nine thousand apartment units, accounting for 6 per cent of the city's total housing and providing accommodations for over thirty thousand of the population. But this statement is not as imposing as it sounds by reason of the fact that the major portion of this housing represents old dwellings and flats acquired by street improvements and dwellings constructed during the housing crisis of the war period, a substantial number of which were temporary in character and not intended for long life. More than half of all this housing is composed of dwelling units of one room and kitchen and two rooms and kitchen.

The tenants of the municipal housing to a very great degree consist of persons who, for economic reasons, have not been able to secure accommodations in either co-operative or private housing. The average income of a tenant family is about $1,250 a year and the average annual rate for a one-room and kitchen unit amounts to about $200. The city has the right to set both initial and future rents, and as a rule the rents are established to cover costs, but allowances are made for poorer tenants in distress. In other words, tenants are either sued or evicted when they *won't* pay rather than when they *can't* pay, a distinction worth noting.

The Real Estate Department of the city controls this housing. A housing deputy, one for each district, collects rents, makes recommendations for repairs, submits names of applicants to the department and exercises general supervision over the dwellings. While periodic inspections occur, the tenants are governed only by reasonable regulations in the use of their apartments.

When Lincoln said, "The Lord must have loved poor people because He made so many of them," he was not confronted with a national housing problem. But the picture has changed. Today, many of those in the field of social work in slum areas have reason to look critically upon large families with little or no means. To illustrate: The scene is the modestly furnished living room of the director of a settlement house in the downtown slum area of a large American city. The time, nine-thirty in the evening. The telephone rings. My hostess, the sympathetic and co-operant wife of the director answers, "Hello. . . . Yes, this is Mrs. Dickens. . . . Oh, good evening, Mr. Flanigan. . . . Yes, yes, you don't say—a boy! How nice, and how is Mrs. Flanigan? . . . I'm so glad, that's fine. . . . What's that? I can't hear. . . . She wants to see me? . . . Of course! I'll be over in a few minutes." She hangs up the receiver. The cheerful manner of the moment before turns to despair as she says, "A new baby across the street; it's her eleventh. She lost two in infancy. Two others are mentally deficient and will later, I'm sure, be wards of society. An older boy is now in a reformatory. The father is out of work and on relief. They all live in two rooms without any inside toilet. Even the water has to be drawn from a tap in the alley shared by five other families. I really don't know what we are going to do with them. They are all undernourished now, babies keep arriving, the situation grows worse and worse. Do you know that we have in this same block two other such families —one with ten children and the other with eleven! They can't get enough to support them even with relief. What do they do in consequence? One family is mixed up in the numbers racket, the other runs a house of prostitution. From our experience here, it's my belief that we can't solve our housing problem until we solve the family problem, and that means less children to burden these poor families. Government subsidy is the only hope; but with families of this size, to provide the necessary rooms for them in decent houses would soon bankrupt the government."

Perhaps the majority of those familiar with similar conditions would hold the same opinion. Their experience is tinged with desperation. They have been too close to reality to look with sentimental favor upon the blessings of a large family in a poverty-stricken environment. They leave the idealizing to the trumpeteering vote-seekers and to those who go down to the slums in slacks! Like the reply made by a woman to a neighbor when asked the subject of the archbishop's sermon, "An' sure, he talked on the joys of married life an' I wish I knew as little about the subject as he does!"

The Swedes think differently about the matter of many children in poor families, and because of the declining birth rate, the government has intervened especially on behalf of this group in society. In 1935 the Riksdag established a loan fund and a rent reduction fund to function together for the purpose of providing suitable housing for large families of low income in towns and other congested urban areas. Additional appropriations have been made in succeeding years and a continuation of the program is a very definite objective today. Under the law the municipalities are required to: (1) provide free land for the building sites; (2) secure first mortgage money up to 60 per cent of the total cost; (3) assume responsibility for any losses of interest on the state loans; (4) furnish 5 per cent of the equity money; and, (5) supervise the construction and manage the projects when completed. The building operations take on the character of a public utility enterprise with state loans acting as secondary credit.

After the buildings are erected the rent reduction feature comes into play. The amount of direct grant for reduction of rent depends on the number of children. In a family of three children (the minimum applicable), the rent reduction is 30 per cent; of four children, 40 per cent; and of five children, 50 per cent. The state then throws up its hands and signifies that it can go no further!

Under this program accommodations are being provided in newly constructed apartment buildings, each housing many families. While recognizing that the single dwelling offers in principle a better living environment for families, the Swedes feel that ownership of an individual house entails burdensome responsibilities which should not be borne by families of very low income. Also it is felt that by erecting multi-family buildings, which can be more readily supervised than single dwellings, there is less opportunity for the accommodations to be used for speculative purposes, thereby defeating the social purpose of the act.

An interesting example of one of the first of these projects was built in 1936 on high ground overlooking the city. The first apartment visited contained three bedrooms, a living room, a small kitchen, and a bathroom. In our excursion through the rooms I noticed an unusual number of beds and cribs, two or three containing very young children. Older children were drifting around. Upon inquiry I found these proud parents had nine offspring. The man was a chauffeur. Without rent reduction he would have paid $22.75 a month but with the government subsidy for the maximum number of children his rent dropped to only half of this amount. Another apartment, occupied by a family with four children, consisted of two bedrooms, a dining alcove in a kitchen, and a bathroom, and rented for $10.82 a month, made possible by a rent subsidy of 40 per cent.

Among the outstanding features of this subsidized housing project were the social facilities. The entire first floor of the largest building was devoted to a children's center under the supervision of trained women. The equipment was modern and complete: there were kitchens for cooking meals for the older children with smaller kitchens for preparing milk formulas for babies; bathrooms; dining rooms; and a number of playrooms for children of different ages. Mothers living in this housing, who were employed in outside work, could leave their young babies at the center and be assured of expert

care of them for the modest charge of about twenty-five cents
a day. Under the same circumstances, older children up to
fourteen years of age could secure hot lunches for a sum
equivalent to fifteen cents a day.

The Swedes are not attempting to solve by these measures
the problem of employment for the mother in a modern age.
That remains a still larger problem. The main purpose behind
the services provided at the children's center is to give poor
mothers, in the family struggle to raise decently many children, an unencumbered chance to add to the family income.
It is recognized by the authorities that, even with government
subsidy, the support of large families with a small income is
difficult, and as a step toward solution of the problem sacri-
ficial measures must be taken by both the parents and the
state. The wife adds her bit to the husband's earnings by
working when able and the state extends a helping hand by
providing the construction loan and rent subsidy for suitable
housing.

According to the provisions of the law, land for this project
was donated by the city. The financing was as follows: 60 per
cent of the construction cost came from a loan secured through
the municipality at 3¼ per cent interest; 35 per cent was loaned
by the state; and the remaining 5 per cent was advanced by a
co-operative housing society which has an interest in this undertaking. The corporation is controlled by the city and the
management is under the Real Estate Department of the city
of Stockholm.

The buildings are three stories in height except the main
one which gains an extra floor by the fall of the ground. The
exterior is severely plain with a white finish. Mildly sloping
roofs, constructed no doubt for economy, accentuate the box-
like appearance of the building units. Simplicity of expression
has been emphasized in the construction. The exterior walls,
ten inches thick, were built of a newly developed insulated

brick now becoming popular in Sweden. Double and triple wood casement windows have been used throughout. The main stairways of light steel had been prefabricated in sections at the mill and then installed. In general, the buildings indicate economical but sound construction: no elaboration, no wastage of materials, and an efficient plan with modern conveniences. The result is a housing project eminently adapted to the needs of the less privileged occupants with large families.

Concerning construction in general in Sweden, we find some interesting developments. Rentals are being based more and more on net floor space, consequently economies in construction and the use of cheaper building materials are eagerly sought. In addition to the innovation of the light insulated brick made of clay and sawdust, we find a material called *gasbetong*, a granulated slate and concrete mixture, in general use. Insulating boards made from the large local supply of pulpwood are finding a ready place in Swedish construction. Native wood, such as birch and beech, are being used extensively as interior finish. I saw the admirable decorative effect of Swedish beech used extensively in a modern school on the outskirts of Stockholm.

The land and construction costs of a dwelling unit are roughly itemized as follows:

	Per Cent
Land (plus street improvements)	10.
Building materials	42.3
Labor	30.5
Plumbing (including installation of gas, water, and sewerage systems)	8.
Heating	7.
Electrical wiring	2.2

Housing standards as they incorporate modern facilities have been constantly improving in recent years in Stockholm.

Gas stoves are now used widely, sinks of stainless steel are in demand, central heating systems are common, and a bathroom to each apartment is no longer a rarity.

In the previous chapter, "Land For Housing," a description was given of the development of the garden suburbs around Stockholm. It is necessary to recall certain features of the municipal land policy which have been responsible for the successful growth of these suburbs. Of the land owned and developed by the city in the outlying sections, building sites, instead of being sold, were leased for a sixty-year period with the privilege of renewal. The motive was to secure cheap land for housing and to avoid the evils of land speculation and increase in prices. The policy has brought the desired results: land prices have not increased; the leasehold plan has not caused hardship to homeowners; the city has been able to maintain high standards of community planning; and, of utmost benefit, families of limited means have had access to improved building sites and assistance in the construction of their homes. In consequence, the garden suburbs, like healthy trees with roots nourished and protected by rich soil, are flourishing. Over nine thousand dwelling units, for the greater part in one-family cottages, have been constructed in the past thirty years, providing accommodations for some fifty thousand persons.

These garden suburbs are laid out in carefully planned communities, some isolated and others grouped together. A striking feature is the preservation of trees, mainly the native evergreens, and this is particularly true in the developments of Nockeby and Traneberg where the dark verdure of pine and spruce provide pleasing and restrained contrast to the colorful houses in these sections. With the forests as one of the main commercial life lines, the Swedes have reason to be mindful of the length of time it takes to grow a tree. "Woodman, spare that tree" is more than mere poetry to them. The developments of Ängby and Tallkrogen are within twenty minutes of the center of Stockholm by bus and electric train, with a commuting fare of about six cents.

Enskedefältet is an interestingly planned development: from the vantage point of a new large school on a wooded bluff, one looks down upon it and follows the length of an open stretch of park. Fanning out on each side lies the housing, composed of small cottages. A main highway skirts one side of the project; another side is protected by the reservation of the abutting ground for shops. This project, by putting on the armament of skillful planning, has been well fortified against the deleterious effects of both commercial and industrial expansion. In consequence, property values are not likely to decline.

The city of Stockholm can be credited with the sponsorship of a unique housing scheme. It appears to have several aliases, "the Stockholm Scheme," "the Magic House," and others. I prefer to call it "self-help" housing because it fulfills literally all that the name applies. The prospective homeowner physically assists in the construction of his house. In 1927, the authorities decided to give a boost to the building of inexpensive small houses in the garden suburbs by persons of slender means, because up to this time only the well-to-do were able to build homes in these areas. The plan was experimental. The city established a credit bureau called "A.S.T." (Aktiebolget Stockholms Tomtrattskassa), from which prospective owners could readily obtain funds at moderate rates for construction. At the same time the city organized in its Real Estate Department a small-house building service. A number of stock plans of small houses were prepared, mechanics employed for skilled labor, and supervisors appointed to give instruction in the simpler operations of building which were to be performed by the "self-help" owners. At the end of the first year the city, by this scheme, had helped some two hundred families to acquire small homes for themselves in the garden suburbs. In succeeding years the city has continued this form of help with the result that today over three thousand families occupy and own houses acquired directly under the municipal "self-help" plan.

The plan works thusly: the prospective homeowner first submits his application to the city. He must meet certain qualification requirements: among others, his yearly income cannot be less than $810 and cannot exceed a sum about double this amount, and he must be able to make a down payment of $78. If his application is approved, he selects from a number of stock plans one that will best meet the living requirements of his family and not exceed his financial capacity. He then chooses his building site from improved municipal land in the garden suburbs and arranges a ground lease with the city on a sixty-year basis. Next, a construction loan is obtained from the city through its credit bureau, A.S.T., up to about 90 per cent of the cost of the proposed house. The remaining 10 per cent equity required will be met by the actual labor to be contributed by the owner. When the financing is arranged and before the construction work starts, the prospective owner is given a pamphlet entitled "Instructions for Building," written in simple language for the novice. After familiarizing himself with that part of the work which he is to perform, a supervisor from the city's office stakes out the house on the ground and then the "self-help" aspect of the plan goes into operation with vigor.

All able-bodied members of the family, and possibly a willing friend or two, start to dig the cellar. Under the circumstances of the owner's regular employment, the family's share of construction can only be done in the late afternoons before nightfall and during week ends. But fortunately the toilers are favored by the lingering light of the long summer days. When

the earth for the basement is excavated the supervisor gives
the lines for the footings and foundation walls and then instructs the family how to mix concrete and lay up the cement-
block basement walls. Next comes the placing of first-floor
joists, the setting up of the prefabricated sectional walls of
wood, partitions dividing the rooms, and finally the roof of
tile. For all of this skilled carpentry work and for the plumbing, heating, and electrical wiring, the city supplies its own
mechanics. When these workmen have finished the family
again carries on with the painting, papering, and other final
touches.

Let us take a Sunday off and see a family at work on a "self-
help" house. I arrived at the site, in one of the garden suburbs,
in the early morning. The building operation stood on the side
of a wooded hill overlooking a rather flat stretch of ground
sprinkled here and there with cottages and little strips of gardens. The resplendent sunshine of a crisp autumn day enlivened the aureoline dress of graceful birch trees fringing a
background of evergreens. The basement walls of the house-
to-be were completed, indicating that the family had labored
diligently through the summer months and had now reached
that stage of their work when skilled help was needed. The
family, gathered together in a tiny two-room cabin just above
the site, were finishing their breakfast. They graciously in-
sisted that I partake of a cup of coffee and a Swedish cake or
two. Conversation was animated—they were in a merry mood
—the carpenters were expected at any moment. In a week's
time their house would be under roof. Soon they could move
in.

The arrival of the carpenters put an end to the frivolities.
Immediate work was ahead for the family; they could assist
as helpers. We all filed out of the cabin.

"Pa" Nisson, the head of the family, was a short, wiry chap
who darted fitfully about the site like a tightly wound me-

chanical mouse. He was here, there, everywhere, but never in any place long enough to accomplish much. Hearing that he was by occupation a teamster for a large brewery in the city, I could vision the little man perched high up on the seat of a brewery wagon, dwarfed to insignificance by a great mass of beer kegs in the rear and a beefy quartet of dappled gray Percherons in front. "Ma" Nisson, on the contrary, was of the build that could hold a Persian host at bay. But toil and middle-age had made slight inroads on her cheery freckled face. The offspring of this oddly mated couple included two daughters in their late teens and a handsome little boy of about ten. One daughter was encumbered with a fiancé, also present, whose preference for leisure at critical work moments was noticeable.

The first operation called for sliding the prefabricated wooden wall sections on rollers down the hill to the building site. "Ma" Nisson was, of course, particularly able in performing this work. She assisted in lifting and swinging the sections around with all the ease of a longshoreman. The daughters also were spirited in their aid. Even the little boy was allowed to assist and I marveled at his youthful strenuousness. In the midst of this activity where was "Pa" Nisson? Well, I noticed that "Pa" had quietly removed himself from the family circle and was earnestly engaged in the tender occupation of pulling tacks out of boards. "Pa" had gotten his hands on an extractor and was having fun with it, and the family probably thought that the work would go faster if he was allowed to entertain himself. After all, when one shoulders beer kegs in and out of cellars all week, there is some excuse for the relaxing occupation of tack-pulling. The fiancé was not in sight!

As the wall sections were rolled down to the building, the carpenters lifted them in place, fitting the sides together and then spiking the bottoms securely to the first floor sill. The work went ahead with dispatch and soon two outside walls of the house were erected. Shortly before noon "Ma" Nisson and the daughters came down from the little cabin carrying beer bottles. All hands knocked off work and gathered in a festive group. Bottles were opened, toasts were exchanged, and for a quarter of an hour the family and the carpenters gave themselves over to simple enjoyment. Work starting again, the two remaining walls rose in place, followed by the erection of the prefabricated interior partitions, and, finally, the setting of the ceiling joists. Work came to an end at sun-down. The carpenters were scheduled to return the next morning and carry on until the tile roof was laid and sash fitted in the windows—in all, a matter of three or four days. The next week end a mason would arrive to build the chimney with the family at hand to mix the mortar and help set in place the prefabricated cement blocks containing the built-in flue sections. At last would come the week end when every member of the family would be given a paint brush—the finishing touches—then the triumphant occupation of the new house.

Truly a saga could be written about this Swedish "self-help" plan. Sagas have eulogized themes of less import. There are many sound reasons supporting the argument that this plan of homeownership for low income workers is preferable to other forms of housing. Let me enumerate a few:

(1) It provides the opportunity for the worker with little cash and much brawn to acquire a home.

(2) It gives the family a worthy objective attainable only as a result of united effort. This very unity of effort tends to knit them closer together into a more homogeneous family.

(3) It provides healthful work in the out-of-doors for all. The Saturday afternoon movie and the Sunday card game or the flexing of the muscles in the automobile hold no lure.

(4) It furnishes a useful knowledge of building construction and the installation of equipment, which knowledge can later be applied in the upkeep of the home.

(5) It demonstrates to the children the value of constructive activity.

(6) It permits the worker to select with greater latitude the place where he desires to live in the free environment of a single house. Merely because of economic circumstances he is not compelled to occupy the middle stall of a long row of two-story houses that possess the architectural variety of a train of freight cars.

(7) It also gives the family some latitude in selecting the type of house plan that will best meet their requirements.

(8) It gives the family a definite attachment to their home. By actually engaging in the construction work the family might be said to build themselves into it. Their affections are incorporated, and therefore they will tenaciously struggle to retain their home through adversity. All of which tends to make them stable members of the community.

Under the "self-help" plan the city is not burdened by any expense. There is no subsidy involved. Of the $78 paid by the applicant as initial deposit, two thirds covers the first year's ground rent, and the other one third takes care of all administrative costs to the city, including the services of supervisors in the field.

There are about eight types of house plans available for selection. One of the three popular types, Type III, has the two bedrooms in the half-story under the roof with the wash basin tucked away in the connecting passage and the water closet secluded in the basement. The laundry seems to serve also for bathing purposes. Type VI is more compact, having all the rooms on one floor. The toilet and wash basin have been placed next to the stairs in a small closet to which will some-day be added a tub or shower and an outside window. Type VII, with three bedrooms on the second floor, is for a larger family. The little combination lavatory-water closet room still remains below. All of these types are provided with hot water

TYPE III

26'
17'-6"

LIVING R   HALL   KITCHEN

PORCH

FIRST FL

BEDROOM   HALL   LAV   BEDR

SECOND FL

STORAGE   LAUNDRY

HEATER   COAL

W.C.

PORCH

BASEMENT

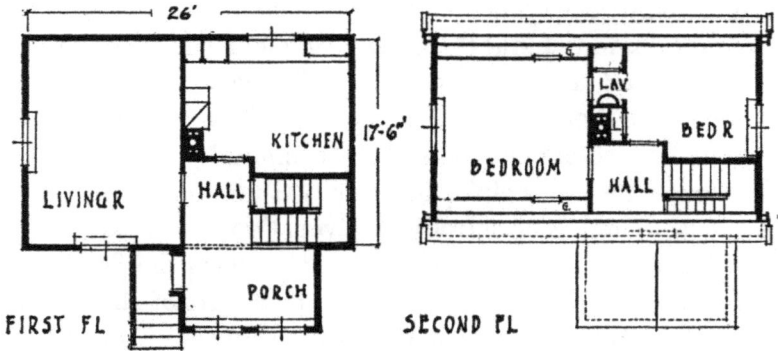

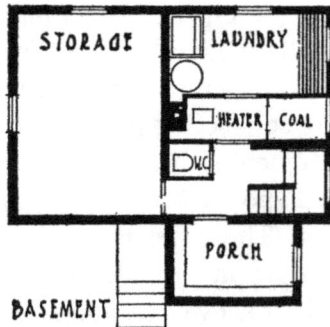

**Popular Types of Plans Used in the "Self-Help"
Housing Scheme of Stockholm (1)**

COPENHAGEN

Court view of a municipal apartment house. The two low sheds in the center provide play space for children in bad weather. Racks for bicycles and facilities for clothes drying and carpet beating are conveniently located

A bedroom in an apartment unit for low income families with many children

STOCKHOLM

A typical kitchen. Note the unusual shape of stainless steel sink

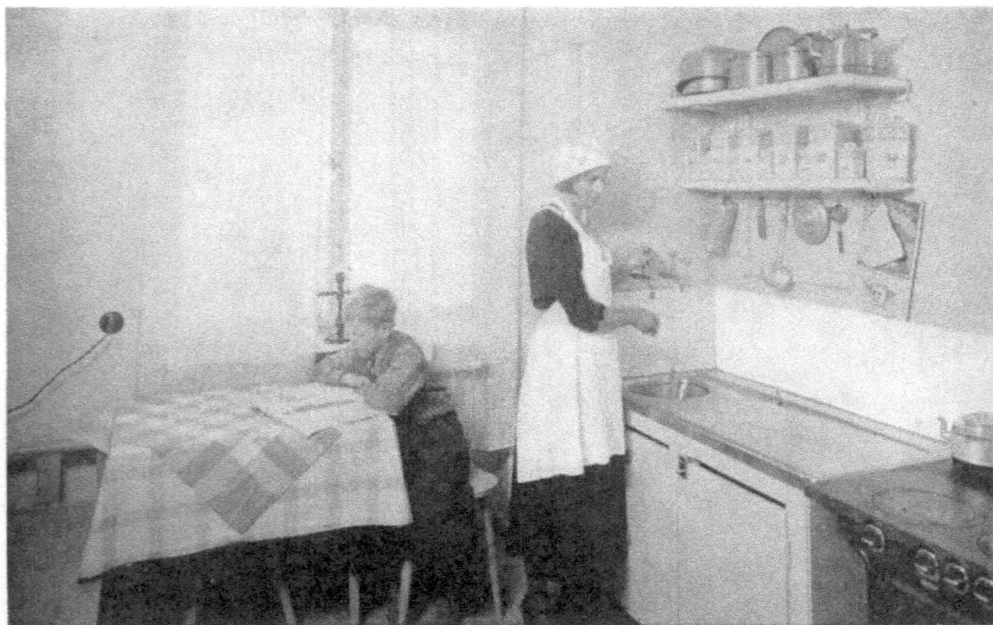

TYPE VII

21'-6"

21'-6"

DINING AL

LIVING R.

KITCHEN

W.C.

HALL

FIRST FL.

BED R.

BED R

BED R

BED R

SECOND FL.

LAUNDRY

STORAGE

C. HEATER

HALL

STORAGE

BASEMENT

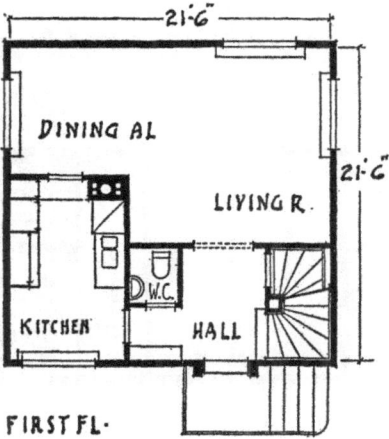

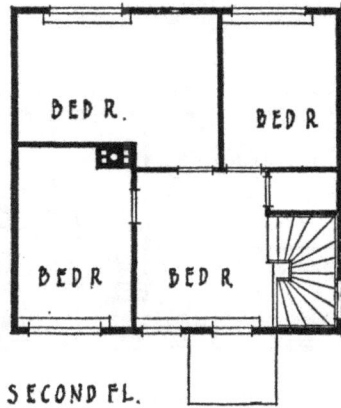

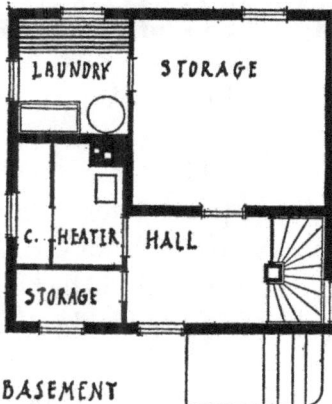

**Popular Types of Plans Used in the "Self-Help"
Housing Scheme of Stockholm (2)**

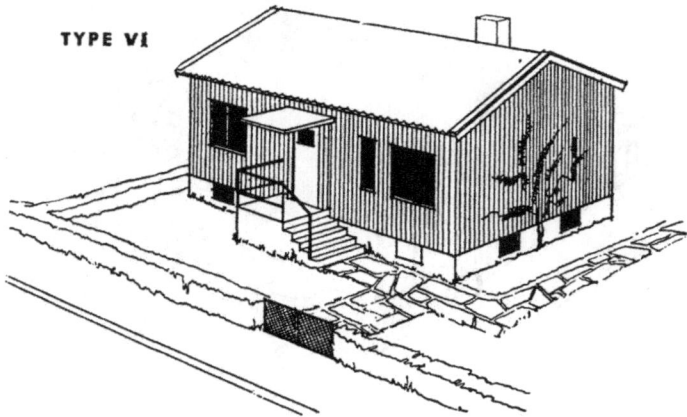

TYPE VI

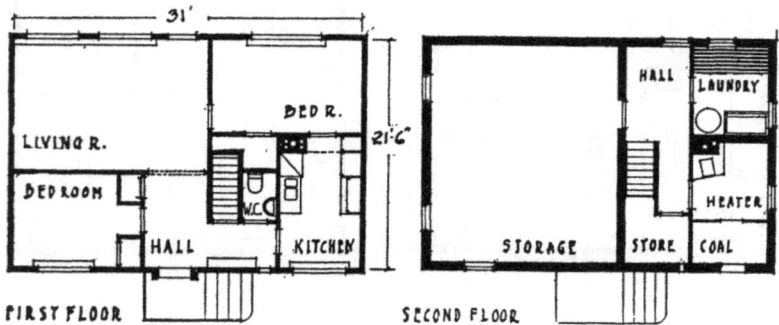

**Popular Types of Plans Used in the "Self-Help"
Housing Scheme of Stockholm (3)**

heating, using coal as the fuel. Cooking is done on gas ranges, and electricity is used for lighting.

The sizes of the lots on which these little houses are placed range in area from 350 square meters as a minimum for the smaller types to 500 square meters for the larger. For the former this means a lot approximately 38 feet by 100 feet, and for the latter a lot approximately 54 feet by 100 feet, or a differently shaped lot 43 feet by 125 feet. On smaller lots the regulations require that there must be a minimum space of 15 feet between houses. In the case of the larger lots the house must be kept at least 15 feet away from each side party line. Many of the minor streets in the planned communities are 24 feet wide between property lines with 4-foot sidewalks.

These little homes have enough ground around them to provide small flower or vegetable gardens. The interiors are usually simple but tastefully furnished. I recall the interior of one where the curtains had been woven by the housewife on a hand loom and the designs were very pleasing. The husband was a policeman for the city.

The municipality of Stockholm so satisfactorily demonstrated the feasibility of this "self-help" method of building small houses for people of modest income that the principal features of the method have been borrowed by private builders. Building contractors with access to credit and to prefabricated materials soon offered the same service to homeowners, building on either municipal or privately owned land. In fact, the majority of small houses built in the garden suburbs on the "self-help" plan have been constructed by private builders. But having pioneered in this method, the city continues its program, constructing on an average of three hundred dwellings a year.

In keeping with the municipal landownership policy of other Scandinavian cities, Gothenburg in Sweden from an early date owned large areas of ground. In 1933 the city held 6,375 acres, chiefly within the city limits. The benefits of this landownership are tersely expressed as follows: "Because of the city's large land holdings, the town plan could be put into effect with greater freedom and the municipal needs more readily met. This has favorably influenced land values. In the newer parts of the city the price of sites for housing has actually decreased while the value of parks, playgrounds, and the like has increased." *

* "The City Board's Opinion and Memorandum, a Survey of Housing

The practice of leasing municipally owned land in Gothenburg is negligible compared to that in Stockholm. In the late 1920's, prospective homeowners in Gothenburg were given the choice of either leasing or purchasing house sites. Later, the city extended to those who had leased land the privilege of buying, and many took advantage of it. The money thus received by the city was put into a special fund from which loans were made to home builders. Today, however, practically all municipally owned land is sold rather than leased. The city recently made available a limited number of lots outside the city to home builders. The sites, leased for a fifty-year period, were equipped with water and sewer facilities, and it was stipulated that the purchasers build and maintain their own roads.

Gothenburg has a metropolitan population of over two hundred and ninety-two thousand persons. Forty-four per cent of the inhabitants occupy a type of housing called *"landslording-husen,"* literally meaning "governor houses." This type consists of a solid-wall first story with two upper stories of frame. Eighty per cent of the apartment units in this housing do not exceed two rooms and kitchen. In the last ten years the *landslordinghusen* type has been the prevailing construction.

From a survey of several thousand apartment units made in Gothenburg in 1930, certain interesting items not usually noted in American surveys were revealed: 12.6 per cent were damp, 7.4 per cent were infested with lice, and 2.1 per cent overrun with rats. Surveys in this country either assume the existence of "wild life" in a slum environment as a normal condition or hesitate to report it on squeamish grounds! The Swedes, on the other hand, with their zeal for cleanliness, stress the point that a well-constructed house must be vermin proof. Other items in this survey indicated that, in general,

Conditions and Policies in Gothenburg, Malmö, Oslo and Helsinki." Published by the Municipality of Stockholm, 1935. (Translated from the Swedish for the purposes of this study.)

modern sanitary facilities were not numerous and that there was much room for improvement.

For many decades Gothenburg struggled against a housing shortage, due mainly to devastating fires. Also, the expanding commerce and trade of this busy port brought an excessive demand for accommodations. The World War intensified this shortage to such a degree that the authorities were compelled to intervene with house building, bringing a measure of relief. But today the density of occupancy in Gothenburg remains greater than in Stockholm, but on the other hand, rents are about a third lower and we find that 70 per cent of the low income group spend less than a fifth of their income for rent.

Due to the prevailing shortage, Gothenburg built its first municipal housing, a few small one- and two-story wooden houses about a century ago. Not until 1919 did the municipality resume its activity by constructing seventy-four three-story apartment buildings of *landslordinghusen* type, containing mainly one- and two-room units. This expenditure of $7,000,000 exceeded even the amount spent for municipal housing by the city of Stockholm. The lowest income group occupies this housing, and poor families with many children are given preference; to a great extent their rent is met by the city's Poor Board.

Between the years of 1917 and 1921, Gothenburg, like other Swedish cities, received direct grants of money from the state for both municipal and private housing construction. Building loans also came from the state, but for the most part they were applied directly to the stimulation of private construction. A city administrative bureau made up of three main departments, finance, real estate, and technical, has controlled and managed the municipal housing.

Malmö, the third largest city in Sweden, with a population of 139,000 persons, has experienced only a slight increase in size in the past decade. As one quarter of the total land area of the city is owned by the municipality, little difficulty has been experienced in carrying out the city plan. As another result of municipal ownership, land prices have been kept down and building construction has been fostered. City-owned land has not been leased for housing purposes to any great extent; instead, the usual method of outright sale is practiced. However, interest in leasehold seems to be gaining favor and this method is being used in the leasing of municipal land for garden colonies and the so-called potato colonies, the former being rented for a ten-year period and the latter on a yearly basis.

Malmö's municipal housing of a permanent nature was confined chiefly to the years 1924–1926, and by 1930 municipal activity had ceased. The city now owns and operates about eleven hundred apartment units, providing living quarters for approximately forty-four hundred persons. Average annual rents for the dwelling units, without central heat, are: for one room and kitchen, $93.60; for two rooms and kitchen, $156.00; and for three rooms and kitchen, $249.00. These rent charges have been set to cover all expenses to the city, and the rent-paying ability of applicants is carefully investigated before the city accepts them. In other words, this is not subsidized housing and does not reach the lowest income group.

In the field of public housing, the city of Helsinki is several laps behind Copenhagen, Stockholm, and Oslo. This retarded position is better understood when it is realized that Finland is predominantly agricultural and that the young republic has apparently felt compelled to direct the greater part of its aid toward colonization in rural areas. But Helsinki has, by its land acquirement policy and the development of its city plan, laid the ground work for a much needed public housing program for its low income groups.

In Helsinki around the year 1900 overcrowding registered

the excessively high index of 208 occupants to each 100 rooms. In the past twenty years that peak has been reduced to 151 occupants, a commendable reduction but still far above the present index figures of 114 for Stockholm, and 115 for Oslo. Even today at least 50 per cent of the inhabitants of Helsinki live under housing conditions where three or more persons occupy a single room.

The city, in a strict sense, owns and controls very little municipal housing. In 1925 it built a few four-story frame structures, containing from four to eight apartment units to a building. Without central heat and plain in design, this housing was erected for families of limited means. In addition, the city acquired approximately forty old dwellings standing on property purchased for parks and street improvements. In 1929 the city participated in the erection of "semi-municipal" apartments by advancing loans for the second mortgage. But as this project was organized as a joint-stock company with ownership shares, it cannot be classified as public housing.

The worker of average income in Helsinki has been confronted with a grave housing problem. He is severely handicapped in securing accommodations in the available joint-stock company housing because the rents are higher than he can afford and because the initial down payment in cash is required for membership. Only some of the older workers, men of forty years or more, with small families and with the savings of many years, can afford the joint-stock company housing. The average income of unskilled workers being around $280 to $466 a year, we see from a glance at the average rents that the ratio of rent to income is excessive:

Average annual rents	Without central heat	With central heat
1 Room (Kitchen or Room)	$ 93	$140
1 Room and Kitchen	140	198
2 Rooms and Kitchen	175	252

When it is realized that over 81 per cent of the inhabitants of Helsinki live in one- and two-room apartments, the problem of the poor family with many children must be recognized as doubly acute.

The town plan of Helsinki has provided for the development of many garden suburbs. One of these suburbs in the northeast section is known as Kottby and contains for the most part frame houses of various types. Our guide through this area was an alert and charming young Finnish woman whose earnest efforts as translator were both commendable and amusing. She would say, "Wait, what es dat word, 'playground'? 'Playground'—let me see." Whereupon she would extract a little dictionary from her handbag and with amazing speed find the Finnish equivalent. "Ah, I have it—'playground'—that is just it! I am studying English; it is good for my work!" The dictionary would disappear into her bag to be hauled forth again every few minutes. I felt a certain sense of shame. The picture ought to have been reversed; I should have been trying to speak her native language; I was shirking a responsibility. But then, I thought, if the choice lay between shame and the effort to master the Finnish tongue, I would emphatically embrace shame.

The city owns the land in Kottby and leases it to homeowners. One- and two-story single houses predominate; there are also a number of semidetached and quadruple houses. One row particularly caught my attention. Built of frame and two stories in height, the exteriors were gaily painted in warm pastel shades with white decorative frames around the window and door openings. We looked at the interior of one of these houses—an unfortunate choice! It was like cutting open a luscious orange and finding the inside withered and dry. The house appeared run down at the heel; paint slithered off the woodwork, shades were badly frayed—mute evidence of straitened circumstances. The interiors of other houses gave quite a different impression, measuring up well to their pleasing exteriors. A room in the basement of one had been quite elaborately arranged as a Finnish bathhouse, with modern heating facilities replacing the simple equipment found in the rural areas.

Persons of various occupations live in Kottby: customs officials, clerks, railroad employees, skilled mechanics, postmen, and others. Rents absorb from 25 per cent to 35 per cent of the family income. Several private housing companies have in the past built dwellings in this suburb, selling the houses in the usual way but leasing the land from the city.

A modified form of the "self-help" housing plan of Stockholm operates in the garden suburbs, but it is quite limited in its extent. For the construction of a small house under the Helsinki plan, a first mortgage loan up to 40 per cent of the construction cost is obtained from the city and the remainder is secured from the prospective homeowner, part in cash and part in labor. Plans are prepared by the city's architectural office, and the builder is selected by the owner with the city's approval.

Some years ago, when authorities on housing in this country were as scarce as heath hens on Martha's Vineyard, a well-known expert startled me by saying, "I'm absolutely opposed to government aid for housing. It's completely unfair. Take England, for instance. Why should a person up in the Lake Region be taxed—and certainly it's a part of his income tax— to help support people living in public housing in London? Answer that. Now listen, I'll tell you something. Just as we have a class of people who must be content with second-hand clothes, so there are people in this world who must live in cast-off housing. That's the natural order of things, young man, and you can't change it. Take it from one who has been in this game a long time and knows." His point of view was unbelievable. Here was the outstanding housing authority of the country not only condemning government aid but in the same breath unfeelingly relegating less privileged humanity to perpetual misery. My social instincts rebelled. It seemed to be putting a ring in the nose of democracy. Housing for the purple-robed, hovels for the wretched—a muddy picture indeed. If today I could find my ex-mentor, who, like the vanishing heath hen, has disappeared from housing circles, I would like to tell him the story of Oslo's experience with public housing. Perhaps it might soften his prejudice.

The World War brought suffering to Norway. By joining the Allies, she lost more than half of her shipping—in proportion, an amount greater than England. In spite of this, after the war she reached down in the bottom of her stocking, took her scanty savings and started to build housing for her people. In 1929, when private enterprise took up the burden of building construction, the municipality of Oslo ceased its efforts, but the extension of municipal credit for housing continued. Today in Oslo, the visitor looks with amazement at the vast number of apartment houses belonging to the municipality and the many others owned by the joint-stock housing societies.

Characteristic of Norway, the local authorities have given more aid to the construction of housing than has the state government. This aid has been in the nature of direct building by the municipalities and support in the form of grants and credit guarantees to public utility societies and private individuals. Immediately following the war, to meet the pressing need for housing, the state established a system of so-called "nonpayable advances" consisting of outright grants of money and loans without interest or amortization charges. These were available to municipal authorities, housing societies, and private builders. To prevent speculation, the government stipulated that the grants should be matched by the municipalities and at the same time fixed the maximum amounts to be spent on the construction of a dwelling unit. As a result of this aid about fifty-five hundred dwelling units were built. The municipalities then assumed the leadership, and in 1922 the state stepped out of the picture.

Almost the entire housing activity of this period was confined to the five largest towns in Norway, and over a half of it was done directly by the municipalities. After 1923, Oslo was the only municipality which continued to build housing to any substantial degree; other towns were forced to discontinue their housing activities because of the financial burden.

During the twenty-year period ending in 1929 when municipal building ceased, the city of Oslo erected some 5,874 dwelling units at a total cost of over $28,000,000. In addition, munificent support was given to joint-stock company housing and private house construction, which received outright grants totaling over $5,000,000 and loans of $16,000,000. Due to the magnitude of these accomplishments, Oslo occupies an outstanding position in the field of Scandinavian housing.

While one- and two-story wooden dwellings predominate in Norway, with some brick buildings in a few of the larger towns, in Oslo the prevailing type is the brick apartment house of from three to five stories, accommodating many families. The dwelling units in the municipal houses consist chiefly of one- and two-room units with kitchen and lavatory. Stoves in living rooms provide heat.

In the Bergensgaten section, not more than ten minutes from the center of the city, I saw a particularly pleasing group of municipal apartment houses. The buildings, all of a clean reddish brick, with restrained cornices and smooth tile roofs, were in their fine proportions suggestive of the English Georgian type. Without the use of expensive materials, the architect had succeeded in producing an aristocratic effect. There was none of the barrenness of institutionalism which so frequently clings to plain buildings. Instead, there was a feeling of quiet charm and dignity. An imposing brick archway, the only real extravagance, introduced us to a spacious landscaped area separating two of the largest buildings of the group. Unadorned but well-proportioned doorways led to the various apartment units. The interiors were simply finished, and the plain furnishings denoted that the occupants belonged to the lower income group.

Rents at Bergensgaten amounted to $10.50 a month for the one room and kitchen units, and $14.25 for units with two rooms. Heat and hot water for domestic use were not included; the tenants use stoves and furnish their own fuel. As the average income of a skilled worker in Oslo falls between $750 and $825 it is seen that the ratio of rent to income, about 20 per cent, is satisfactory.

We stopped in front of another large group of buildings a dozen blocks away from Bergensgaten. By contrast to the simplicity of the last place, here stupendous efforts had been made to attain elegance in formal dress. Due to the rising grade the buildings were on two levels and a monumental stairway, starting at the street, ascended pompously to a terrace above, halting in front of an apartment building that possessed all the official embellishments of a town hall. Suggestive of Tennyson's "Maud," the effect was: "Faultily faultless, icily regular, splendidly null!" As a solution to a theoretical problem in design it might have merited attention, but as a practical feature in an economical public housing project it was decidedly *de trop*. I fancied I could almost hear a passing citizen indignantly mutter, "Wasting taxpayers' money!" And in this case I would be compelled to agree.

The city abounds in creditable examples of municipal housing. To designate a few of the larger projects in the outlying sections, I might mention the picturesque grouping of two-and-a-half-story brick apartment buildings at Ulleval Haveby, which in their symmetrical proportions and cornice lines again follow the English Georgian. As a matter of fact, much of Oslo's housing shows the English influence, and with the close trade and cultural ties between Norway and England this is rather natural. At Tassen, still farther out, one sees a number of colorful two-story frame houses, each containing two dwelling units. And not to be overlooked is the impressive housing abutting Torshov Park, built in 1920 with municipal aid.

As a hangover from an earlier land buying policy, the municipality of Oslo still owns some land within the city limits but the amount is small. Unlike the other Scandinavian capitals, Oslo is not now engaged in land acquirement for future use. The lack of such a policy is being felt. A leading official expressed it to me in this way: "We have no municipal land acquirement policy like Stockholm's. It is most regrettable, because the city is unable to exercise control over new developments in outlying areas. Also the city's boundaries are too small: too many persons employed in the city live outside the city's jurisdiction. The city loses the taxes."

After the year 1900 many Norwegian municipalities made extensive purchases of land in the outskirts of urban centers. They were able thereby to accumulate sufficient reserve to provide land sites for the accelerated house building of the postwar period. At that time sites were leased on easy terms. Today in Oslo, of the remaining land, sites are usually leased to joint-stock housing societies and individuals for a period of sixty years with the privilege of renewal for another thirty years. The land rent is 4½ per cent of the site's value, which varies in different sections of the city. The right of condemnation does not exist and local authorities are compelled to purchase land by agreement.

The rents in the municipal housing have been fixed without regard to building costs, and as a whole they account for only 50 per cent of these costs. Loss to the city from delin-

quent rents has been insignificant. Administrative costs to the
city amount to 3.3 per cent of the rent.

Municipal housing activity in Oslo has appreciably relieved
the housing problem for the lower income groups, but it has
not solved it. Overcrowding still exists, particularly in the
smaller room units of one and two rooms. As in Sweden, the
problem acutely concerns itself with the poorer families with
many children who cannot afford to secure quarters with
enough rooms to accommodate their families properly. But
the Norwegians have an acute sense of social well-being.
They also have courage and persistence. If the solution of this
problem requires another dip into public funds it is not likely
that these people of Viking stock, inured to the necessity of
sacrifice, will hesitate.

ALLOTMENT GARDENS

The municipalities of Copenhagen, Stockholm, and Helsinki have made provision for allotment gardens or garden
colonies. In some cases the allotments are located in or near
the central sections of the city, but as a rule they occupy land
in the outlying areas. Their function is to provide city dwellers of modest means with an opportunity for access to the
soil to grow flowers and a few vegetables and to enjoy an en-
riched living usually reserved for those in better economic
circumstances. The allotment gardens are utilized only during
summer months.

Copenhagen is fairly peppered with these little gardens on
vacant land in the residential districts. I shall not forget my
abrupt introduction to one on a Sunday afternoon. I had just
completed photographing a "luxury flat" built by private industry for tenants of means. This lean five-story building,
stretching to seeming infinity, was horribly infested on its garden side with clinging balconies as replete as fish eggs on a
water plant. Just across the street, half buried in shrubbery, I

spied a tiny red cottage of an allotment garden. No bigger than a one-car garage, its many oversized white framed windows reduced the scale of the little house to the semblance of a toy. I felt a desire to lift up the roof and peer inside. On a miniature porch about the size of a picnic cloth sat an elderly couple, and at their feet, on a mere pinch of ground, were the flowers and vegetables. Here was contrast! The man-reared apartment house, its head in the clouds, and the earth-bound cottage, close to the breath of flowers. Here, too, was democracy: where else but in Denmark would one see such extremes of living being allowed to exist side by side.

The majority of these little summer cottages in allotment gardens are of only one or two rooms. Without permanent locations designated on the city plan of Copenhagen, the garden colonists are subjected unfortunately to a nomadic existence because, if the land is needed for building purposes, the colonists must vacate and start afresh on some other ground. A genuine hardship results. Despite this, allotment garden living is so popular with the public that occasionally impecunious applicants go to great lengths to erect little cottages, occasionally even utilizing the wooden crates of imported American automobiles.

Sweden borrowed the unplanned allotment garden idea from Denmark and developed it into planned garden colonies. The allotment garden movement did not get underway with vigor in Sweden until the beginning of the century. In Stockholm the movement was pushed by the Allotment Garden Association and it was due to their energy and wisdom that the planning of definite locations for the garden colonies was adopted. The association was also able to have a regulation enforced requiring that the little cabins or cottages conform to certain standard plans and designs. Both were excellent innovations in the irregular and haphazard allotment garden scheme of Copenhagen.

There are allotment gardens in all of the large Swedish cities. Stockholm has the greatest number, with the city of Malmö not far behind. During the World War period allotment gardens experienced a great expansion, due to the food shortage. In some instances the municipalities rent garden land directly to individuals, but in most cases the land is rented to co-operative societies, which distribute plots to their members. In Stockholm it is possible to obtain a lease varying in length from ten to twenty-five years.

The original purpose of the little cottage on an allotment plot was to serve as a temporary shelter from the rain or, in an emergency, as a place to spend the night. But from the pristine idea of the tiny patch of ground and the temporary shelter, the trend is now toward more permanently built cottages and larger allotment areas so that families can more comfortably occupy them throughout the entire summer.

In Helsinki, garden colonies became a part of the permanent city plan around 1920, shortly after the establishment of Finnish independence. Today five of these colonies are located in different sections of the suburbs on city-owned ground. Each provides accommodations for about three hundred families. And more colonies are being placed on the city plan. The municipality is the landlord, renting small plots for a sum of from $4.00 to $5.00 for the summer season. The lease runs for a period of twenty years, and plans of the small cottages, erected by the tenant, must be approved by the city.

The garden colony in the Kottby section of Helsinki is quite pretentious in its layout and equipment; Helsinki attaches a good measure of importance to the allotment garden scheme. The site plan is formal. Cottages are supplied with electricity and piped water, and modern toilet facilities are provided for cottages in groups. A community hall has been erected by the city in the center of the colony, and another unique feature furnished by the city is the free instruction in gardening. A

STOCKHOLM

A typical living room and, below, a play room in the social center of a municipally sponsored apartment house for large families of low income

Municipally sponsored housing for large families of low income. Rentals are based on floor space and the number of children in the family

STOCKHOLM

Enskedefältet, one of the newer garden suburbs. Its property values are protected by skillful planning

male gardener instructs the adults and a woman gives lessons to the children.

It would be difficult to picture a more attractive scene than the panorama which these Scandinavian garden colonies afford; each small garden patterned with its miniature cottage, the colorful flowers, and the national flag high overhead. It is doubtful whether a municipality could secure any greater value for its population by the expenditure of a limited amount of money than by investing the available funds in garden colonies, since both the health and the morale of the people are improved. Especially is this true when the gardens are placed within reach of families with little to spend for leisure activities.

Through the eyes of a Swedish writer, we glimpse the role played by one of these small allotment gardens in the summer life of a Stockholm industrial worker:

"Now is the time of climbing roses, of many-bloomed blue delphiniums, of larkspurs, of white, pink, crimson, and purple hollyhocks. Peter is wading knee-deep, breast-high, in a sea of perfumed color. His pants are water-splashed, his shoes muddy, but he doesn't mind, this man. He has turned up his shirt at the neck, and now he bends his back to his task with a will. It would be strange if he couldn't make this koloni look like something he has in his mind's eye, now, wouldn't it?

"Around noon he sights Hanna over on the highway. She comes lugging a big basket covered with a white napkin. Her face is all smiles as she proceeds down the path that leads to the koloni. 'Hello, Peter!' she cries, 'Are you hungry?'

"Peter sticks that spade of his into the ground and straightens his back. He emphasizes the movement so that anyone might see that he has been working hard. He glances around at what he has done. Then he stands waiting.

" 'My, haven't you done a lot!' Hanna exclaims as she enters through the gate.

"Peter gives a satisfied sniff. 'I dug up those hollyhocks there that didn't fit in,' he remarks.

"She glances vaguely at the flower bed. 'Ua-a-ah—I see. You've planted some carrots, too, somewhere, haven't you? And spinach. You know, spinach is good for your health. It has iron in it.'

"They step into the tiny bungalow where Hanna begins to unpack the basket. 'Meatballs,' she says, smiling.

"Peter sits down and slaps the dust off his trousers. He casts a glance out over the sun-flooded garden where a bee is droning by over the nodding flowers. And all at once he feels very solemn, as though he had been sitting in a church, listening to a moving sermon. A warm whiff of air brings into the room a heavy sweet scent. Everything is so quiet. Sunday stillness. The wind's rustling among swaying boughs. And peace. . . ." *

---

* Reprinted from *Our Daily Bread*, by Gösta Larsson, with special permission of the Vanguard Press, New York.

3. HOUSING SOCIETIES

AN OUTSTANDING FEATURE OF POSTWAR HOUSING in Scandinavia has been the extraordinary growth of the so-called public utility housing societies. We in America commonly think of the term "public utility" as applying exclusively to privately owned but publicly supervised industry. In Scandinavia as in the rest of Europe, however, the term "public utility" also applies to private and semi-private housing organizations which have received encouragement through special legislation and governmental aid in various forms.

The most prevalent type of public utility housing is the co-operative, which has taken two general forms: (1) that in which members acquire ownership of dwelling units, whether the dwelling units be in multi-family buildings or single houses; and (2) that in which members acquire the privilege of occupying dwelling units, the ownership remaining in the hands of the organization. In turn, the latter form has developed in two different directions which will be described later. Another type of public utility housing society is the limited dividend joint-stock company organized by persons, institutions, or industrial organizations for the purpose of providing low rent housing accommodations. In the varied forms of public utility housing there is a wide range in the extent of the social purpose. At one end of the pole is the co-operative housing society based on Rochdale principles and at the other end is the joint-stock housing society with limited dividends.

Outside of the bounds of public utility are the Finnish joint-stock lodging societies with unlimited dividends. Perhaps we might liken the social motive content in these different societies to wine and the profit motive content to water and then, starting with the Rochdale co-operative society as wine, we would gradually dilute with water until we ultimately obtained the extreme form of the Finnish joint-stock lodging society, which is actually private enterprise. In using this simile it is not the purpose to disparage the profit motive in housing. After all, in a democratic society there are many who think the straight beverage too heady and prefer to have it cut with water, while others are suspicious of any drink that is not drawn from a well. So it is with the variations found in housing societies. The advantages gained have without question demonstrated the value of diversification in the housing field.

In Scandinavia a substantial number of housing societies, recognized by their respective governments as public utilities, were in existence before the World War, and when the housing need became acute they were in a position to develop a large number of building projects sponsored and financially assisted by the public authorities. Because of the completeness of their organizations and the experience behind them, their governments, instead of doing the work themselves, preferred to let these housing societies be the instrument for supplying housing accommodations for a considerable part of the population. In consequence, the activities of the housing societies assumed importance in the postwar era. Even when government aid was decreased, many of these societies, because of the fact that their position had become well established, were able to continue their activities with little abeyance. For example, the Workmen's Co-operative Housing Society in Copenhagen, organized in 1912, has shown a steady growth, and today it occupies an enviable position in Denmark's capital. Other societies, starting since the war have shown phenomenal development. The K.A.B. society * in Copenhagen has reached the leading position in Denmark, and the H.S.B. society † in Stockholm, organized as late as 1923, is today the largest in Sweden, with branches in over sixty cities.

In today's troubled existence, made more precarious by the threatened extinction of mankind either by war or the insatiable hunger of insects, there are fortunately a few remaining certainties on which we can rely. We can be reasonably sure of finding empty coal bins or oil tanks in our cellars at the end of winter, if not before; we know that we can expect to see Florida license plates on cars and trailers migrating northward in the spring and southward in the fall; we know we must make allowances for ingratitude from almost any quarter. And finally, there is the certainty of periodically seeing in the newspapers some nabob's disconsolate protest against government aid for housing. This latter certainty will be in evidence as long as houses are built for human occupancy, which of course brings us to the millennium. Recently I saw this headline in a metropolitan daily: "Government Housing Called Unsound by President of Home Builders." In another three months some other disgruntled objector will crash the headlines. These blasts are as regular and evenly spaced as the spoutings of Old Faithful in Yellowstone Park. Underneath the headlines I read, "New Alantus, May 5th. At a meeting of the Board of Homebuilders the incoming President said, 'In my first public statement let me declare that I am utterly opposed to government subsidy for housing. In the first place it is un-American—it is tinged with a European "ism." We don't want it, because we have a different system here. It is well to remind ourselves of the principles laid down in the Farewell Address of the Father of our Country. He said that the one

---

* See pp. 111 ff. for details of organization.
† See pp. 125 ff. for details of organization.

way to preserve government credit was to use it as sparingly as possible. There is no other way to interpret this utterance than by considering it in the same way we regard a spare tire —that is, something to be kept for an emergency. He stated that it was legitimate to use this credit to prepare for threatened danger. We can rightfully believe that he had in mind only bona fide governmental subsidies such as the building of battleships, the erection of post-offices, the extension of national parks, the building up of our merchant marine, the development of airway lines in South America and many other patriotic undertakings which contain far-flung significance. But he certainly never intended that public money should be squandered on such unprofitable enterprises as housing for the low income groups. He would have opposed such wastefulness and I will take my stand on this question at the side of the Father of our Country.

'In the second place government subsidy completely depraves the individual who is unfortunate enough to have to live in a subsidized house. It does something to him from which he can never recover. On occasions I have had to drive through the slums of my home town and let me say to some of you, fathers of children, that there is no more gratifying sight than the determined look on the faces of some of those ragged urchins undergoing the hardships of adversity that will later fit them for public life in our great nation. It is inspiring— haven't many of our most distinguished mayors come out of the slums? Had those persons at the tender age of six months been removed from the slums and put in subsidized housing, we all know that the spark of genius would have been extinguished forever and they would have grown up without zeal for public service.

'In the third place, subsidized housing puts an unjust burden upon the man who owns a decent house. He has fought his way to the top of the heap and then the government turns around and taxes him to help the weaklings at the bottom of the heap. That's unjust because it's un-American! What concern is it to the hard-working home owner how slum dwellers live? That is their problem to solve. And further, the man living in a decent house is burdened with enough expenses. He has installment payments to meet on his automobile, radio, refrigerator, washing machine, vacuum cleaner, electric razor and a score of other household articles. He can't afford to be taxed to support a subsidy. As I said at the beginning, I am definitely opposed to government subsidy because it is unsound. Now, I have a plan for housing the low income group which is so practical that it will make federal housing superfluous. It won't cost the government a cent. It is based on the sound business principle of "cash and carry" with the self-service features of our sturdy pioneer ancestors replacing the installation of expensive utility facilities. . . .' The President closed his remarks by describing government financing of housing as 'chimerical and extravagant.' "

The absurd reasoning in pronouncements of this kind drip from the daily press like occasional oil from a crankcase and merit as little attention. To apply the specific term "subsidy" to the entire field of government aid to housing is inaccurate and misleading, since this aid assumes many shapes of which subsidy may or may not be a part. This loose use of the term is frightening to the layman who visualizes great sums of public money being hurled into a bottomless pit. Dr. Johnson took exception to Garrick's portrayal of Hamlet in the ghost scene and Boswell inquired, "Sir, wouldn't you show the same degree of terror if you saw your father's ghost?" "Certainly not," replied Johnson, "If I did, I might scare the ghost!" Overplaying subsidy is like scaring the ghost.

In this matter of government aid for housing, if we examine the various forms used in the Scandinavian countries during the postwar period it will be seen that, while subsidy played an important part, it has been only one of many forms used to stimulate housing construction. Government aid has been extended in such various ways as the following:

First, subsidies in two general forms: (a) Initial or lump sum payments for a part of the building cost, representing outright grants of money without expectancy of repayment, or (b) annual outright grants to cover part of the annual charges.

Second, extension of government credit facilities by state and municipality, acting together or separately: (a) Simple guarantees by public authorities that interest and amortization charges will be regularly paid. For this purpose the governments usually set up special reserve funds or independent credit institutions such as the Small Holdings and Dwellings Bank in Norway, the State Dwelling Loan Fund in Sweden, and the Mortgage Bank of the Building Industry in Finland, the last two organized on co-operative lines. And, as a supplementary provision, the governments at times secured the participation of insurance companies with large capital resources, inviting them to invest part of their funds in construction loans guaranteed by the governments. (b) The governments assumed responsibility for part payment of interest and, in some cases, for redemption of principal. (c) The governments assumed responsibility for the entire financial operation, granting loans on their own account.

Third, tax exemption: Exemption from taxes and supertaxes on real property for a given length of time, and in some cases exemption of stamp and registration duties levied by the state on land purchase, bond issues, and other documents relating to mortgages. In Denmark, for example, tax exemption is in force up to the year 1943 on buildings of a social character, which of course include the buildings of the co-operative societies. This exemption has been most beneficial, amounting to about 3 per cent of the building cost, and is duly reflected in reduced rents.

Fourth, building sites provided by the municipalities at low cost: From their land reserves municipalities have been able to supply desirable building sites to the recognized public utility societies at reduced prices for the construction of housing. The extension of this favor has enabled municipalities to impose certain restrictions as to the use of the buildings constructed and the rents to be charged.

DENMARK

"And be we poor and lowly
Yet are we sons of kings
And higher than the eagle
Hope may spread out her wings."

Thus sang the great Danish patriot, Grundtvig, extolling a democratic principle that "only he who believes each human soul has eternal life is able, without self-delusion, to recognize kinship in his fellows, however poor and ignorant they may be." * Denmark is a nation of co-operatives, and co-operation of the Rochdale type is particularly and properly expressive of democracy because it is based on an equal right of members to participate in the organization, and an equitable sharing in the benefits accruing. Housing is only one strand in the whole co-operative fabric which in Denmark has been woven in a singularly interesting pattern.

In the year 1844 two significant events took place, seemingly of no relation to each other. In the village of Rødding, in northern Slesvig, the first Danish folk high school was founded and at the same time in the village of Rochdale in Lancashire, England, a few flannel weavers banded together

---

* Holger Begtrup, *The Folk High Schools of Denmark,* trans. Humphrey Milford (London, Oxford University Press, 1936).

and formed a co-operative society, based on a new set of principles of co-operation for the distribution of consumer goods. Succeeding years brought a slow but steady increase in the establishment of folk high schools in the rural areas of Denmark, while in England co-operative societies based on the Rochdale principle multiplied extensively. The education gained at the folk high schools by the young men and women of the rural areas quickened their mental perception and made them responsive to enlightened ideas. Not many years rolled by before agricultural Denmark was being told about the progressive achievements of co-operation in England, and as early as 1851 feeble and unsuccessful attempts were made to introduce it in Denmark. But it was not until 1866 that a real foothold was secured by the founding of the Society of Working Men in Thisted Town, based on the same principles of co-operation used at Rochdale. The movement spread slowly, receiving its early impetus in the rural areas.

After 1880, as a result of the nation's adjustment to a drastic change in agricultural economics, the co-operative movement took a new step forward and increased its pace until today we find co-operation a widespread and deeply rooted practice in the life of the Danish people. Many educators in Denmark consider the influence of the folk high schools responsible in no small measure for the remarkable growth of co-operation. Therefore, with the background of co-operative practice wherein people had learned to work together for a common good in the economic field, it was not difficult for them to extend the idea to living together on a co-operative housing basis.

During the housing crisis period of the World War, co-operative and other public utility housing societies in Denmark were singled out for special encouragement by the passage of favorable legislation, and this brought a marked increase in construction. The government either made loans to co-operative housing societies or granted them credits. The loans bore interest at 4 per cent and were issued up to 90 per cent of the building cost. Subsidies were granted to co-operative societies: some on a basis of 10 per cent of the building cost and others as high as 20 per cent with the stipulation, however, that the government exercise control over the renting and selling of the building. To further stimulate construction, in 1922 the government created a State Housing Fund for the explicit purpose of extending second mortgage loans to housing societies and private persons. These loans usually ranged between 30 per cent and 40 per cent of the building cost with the stipulation that loans made on a building could not exceed 85 per cent or 90 per cent of the cost. Local authorities were required by the state to deposit a guarantee equivalent to one half the amount of the loan from the State Housing Fund. This state fund, during the five years of its existence, was responsible for two thirds of all the housing erected, the major portion of which was built by the housing societies. The principal beneficiaries were the more highly paid workers and the salaried employees. On the other hand, because the state controlled the design of houses erected and directed the use of the ground, standards were raised, and this in turn was beneficial to housing in general. Still another advantageous provision of the government was the deferring of payment on State Loan Funds. This related particularly to the larger projects erected in Copenhagen and resulted in a certain small reduction in rents.

A native of Arizona once told me that there were two schools of thought in his state: one school believed that rattlesnakes were on the increase and the other school was of the opinion that they were on the decrease. He said the issue had never been settled one way or the other. In the same way, each of the two principal types of co-operative housing has adherents; it is impossible to accept one as preferable in all respects and disregard the usefulness of the other. Firstly, there is the orthodox Rochdale type of society conducted according to the precepts of the Rochdale pioneers: that is, every tenant a member, one vote only allowed to each member, and the membership owning and controlling the organization. Secondly, there is the modified type of co-operative housing society which assumes more of the character of a limited dividend housing company with the control vested in the society rather than in the membership. There are advantages and disadvantages in both types. In the first or Rochdale type, the tenant members derive certain benefits which are not to be found in any other form of housing. There is instilled in them a feeling that they are joint owners of an organization and that they are actually doing something for themselves—helping to solve their own living problem. And by following the Rochdale principles, which include return of savings (termed "profits" in private business) to the tenant members, they are able to secure their dwelling accommodations at a cost as much as 20 per cent lower than in the modified co-operative. In comparison with housing built by private enterprise the savings are even greater.

But this very ownership and self-government by the tenant members calls for stable residence. Consequently it is chiefly adapted to those tenants whose employment permits them to settle more or less permanently in a particular location. Also, due to the absence of the profit motive with the resulting elimination of opportunities for speculating in buying and selling of dwelling units, it becomes imperative that the Rochdale society erect its building projects economically as to materials, labor, interest and amortization charges, and cost of land.

The principal advantage of the modified type of co-operative housing, which has reached a place of importance within the last decade, lies in the fact that it offers the occupants a greater mobility than could be obtained under the Rochdale type. As the occupants have little or no voice in the control of the organization, there is not the same feeling of responsibility for management. They are in a position to maintain a more temporary residence. Being recognized legally as limited dividend companies, with a maximum dividend of 5 per cent paid to stockholders, these societies are in a favorable position and are able to secure construction money on advantageous terms. Consequently their rents are slightly lower than those prevailing in private housing, but not so low as in the Rochdale co-operatives. Salaries of tenants occupying the modified co-operative housing are higher than those in the Rochdale type. In the different forms of modified co-operatives, it is usual for the tenants to become stockholders and regardless of whether they remain as occupants of a society's building, they may retain ownership of their stock. Also, it is possible for outsiders to acquire stock and secure a voice in the management. Neither of these practices are permissible in the Rochdale co-operatives. Where a central society of the modified type owns several "daughter" buildings, as a rule the tenants in each building elect committees which participate with non-dwelling members in the general election of the administrative board of the central society. Therefore the influence of the tenant members is limited and in no sense as potent as that of the members in a Rochdale co-operative society. Nevertheless, the modified type with its centrally organized control and loose membership attachment, operating in the field of public utility housing, satisfies a definite need of a certain part of the population living under modern conditions and is a useful supplement to the orthodox Rochdale type.

One morning a middle-aged couple appeared at the breakfast table of our hotel in Copenhagen. Brief introductions took place, the newcomers using a hybrid cockney accent to explain that they hailed from Australia and were "seeing" Europe for the first time. When I heard this and looked at the man's weatherbeaten face, I conjectured that a trip through Europe for him must be in the nature of a blessed relief from the daily round of fighting bush fires and skirmishing with aborigines. At least, it was pleasant to thus colorfully clothe the home-life of my new acquaintance in gentle retaliation for some of the questions that had been addressed to me by Europeans, bearing on wild life in New York City revolving around Indians, buffaloes, and gangsters. "I say, what's worth seeing in this town?" he asked. "How long are you staying?" I inquired. "Until tomorrow noon. Paris is calling and we must keep up with our schedule." "Well," I rejoined, somewhat appalled by the thought of a tourist allowing only a day and a half to "see" Copenhagen and going through it with the interest an ambulance driver on a hurry call takes in shop windows, "You had better go straight to Tivoli and spend most of your time there. Tivoli is the famous amusement park in the center of Copenhagen. It has in it every known and unknown gambling device, but the funny thing is you don't really gamble. When you win they give you a 'souvenir,' which might be anything from a stuffed teddy-bear to a walking stick. When you get tired watching the roulette wheels spin round and the little white balls dancing into lucky slots, you can try your skill smashing kitchen crockery. Oh, it's lots of fun and you'll like it." I could see real interest beginning to light up his face, so I continued, "And then, in the evening, go to Vivex for a superb dinner. Everybody dines at Vivex; it's the thing to do. After that, take in a night club show at the National Scala." He thanked me profusely for the advice and his wife expressed her gratitude. I had packed the waking hours of their brief stay with possibilities; he could now thumb his nose at that scourge of tourists, ennui. He breezed

out of the dining room like a man liberated from a dungeon
—Copenhagen was good for twenty-four hours!

At a time when so much emphasis is being put on the advantages of a democratic form of government, it seemed unfortunate that this couple felt no desire to linger in a country
where they would have seen democracy working at its best.
This criticism is no reflection on their nationality; they might
just as well have been American tourists. I ran into two such
galloping travelers from the United States on the boat plying
from England to Denmark. The jittery couple, suffering from
frayed nerves and "mean feet," as some Southern folk aptly
describe it, had just raced past the three-quarter milepost
and were tearing down the home stretch of their tour. They
proudly produced their itinerary, made up undoubtedly by
some disengaged marathon runner temporarily employed in
the travel bureau of their home town. It was a challenging
document. No intrepid explorer would have lightheartedly
undertaken the European tour arranged for this couple. They
used the customary expression of "did" for past sight-seeing.
They "did" Stratford-on-Avon in a morning. They "did" York
Minster in less than two hours and "covered" Lincoln, Ely,
and Peterborough cathedrals in the afternoon. In London
they "did" Westminster Abbey, the National Gallery, the
Tower, British Museum, and the Parliament Buildings in a
day. They "missed" St. Paul's Cathedral because it was not
"on" their itinerary and this was a great blow because fellow-
travelers, picked up here and there, had been asking "You
saw St. Paul's Cathedral, of course?" and they had to be brave
and frank and tell why they hadn't seen it. They admitted that
the pace was wearing and looked forward to a rest on the
boat home. Yes, it was a wonderful experience; their view-
point had been greatly enlarged and they had much to tell
their friends at Zanesville. They liked Hampton Court because it was so convenient to shops and theatres and then,

too, the beds were so comfortable. I asked if they "did" the Trossachs. No, they replied, but they had learned the Lambeth Walk!

To return to Denmark, if we are to understand the nature of co-operative housing, it is necessary to go behind the structural organization of the societies and try to catch the spirit of Danish democracy which has provided a favorable environment for their growth.

In the first place the Danes, in demonstrating equality, show an unusual degree of respect for personality. Personal worth is not necessarily made subservient to material worth, and service to society takes on an element of classless appreciation. The task that an individual performs in his humble way according to the best of his capacity is recognized as valuable to society. Grundtvig beautifully expressed the ideal of Danish equality in one of his well-known songs:

> "Far more of those metals so white and so red
> Find others by digging and selling.
> We Danes, though, can point to everyday's bread
> In even the lowliest dwelling—
> Can boast that in riches our progress is such
> That few have too little, still fewer too much."

It is illuminating to watch the little ceremony that is enacted in a restaurant when a distinguished-looking person, who might easily be a member of Parliament, prepares to depart after a sumptuous meal. With an easy show of courtesy the waiter hands the guest his silk hat and cane. Then follows a friendly handshake while pleasant words of farewell are exchanged, and as the guest leaves the restaurant, he tips his hat to the waiter. All very friendly and truly democratic. The attitude of the guest implies: "Your job as a waiter and my job as a parliamentarian are both necessary to society; as citizens of the state we are equal. My intellectual capacity may be

STOCKHOLM

Skilled mechanics employed by the city erect the prefabricated walls of a "self-help" house

A typical "self-help" house in the garden suburbs. Construction plans are supplied as a part of the service of the municipality

A family is shown at work on their "self-help" house after receiving instructions from one of the city's supervisors

HELSINKI

Two-story frame municipal apartment house

OSLO

Municipal housing

greater than yours, and according to the way of the world society pays me more generously for my services, but this difference has no bearing on our relative worth as individuals."

When material worth yields its commanding position to human worth, the former loses something of its phosphorescent glow and is less eagerly sought after. Then strange things are likely to happen. In the environs of Copenhagen I was shown a new house constructed from funds raised by a grateful public and offered as a gift to a retired and much-beloved prime minister of Denmark in recognition of his meritorious services to the state. The house was not a pretentious affair by any means. It was of ordinary size with a modest amount of ground around it. The ex-minister replied to the public that he would gratefully accept the house as his home while he lived, but that upon his death he wanted it to be returned to the state. According to general standards this might be considered unbusiness-like, but in the light of Danish social philosophy it was not a surprising action.

O. Henry quaintly remarks that when women without sealskin coats grow kind to their husbands, then winter is at hand. Some of the unusual sights in Copenhagen signify that the democratic spirit is at hand. I have in mind one of the city's parks, several blocks long, located in a central area. Recreation and rest facilities had been provided for all ages: sand lots for the small children, swings and climbing apparatus for those slightly older, a spacious wading pool for youngsters, a large open grass area for kite-flying and general play, and finally, a quiet lawn area appropriately separated and equipped with numerous benches for the older people. Surrounding the entire park there were three different types of housing in four- and five-story buildings: municipal apartment buildings for the low income group, co-operative apartments for the middle income group, and private "luxury flats" for the upper income group. No segregation, and the occupants of each type looking out upon and sharing the facilities of the common park without regard to their relative economic position.

It is interesting to glance at a typical (1937–1938) Danish national budget:

	Per Cent
Civil List, Parliament, and Foreign Office	2.0
Defense	11.9
Internal Administration	9.8
Expenditure Connected with Trade and Industry	14.6
Social Purposes	32.7
Public Education	13.7
Health	3.8
Miscellaneous	11.5

At once we see that the largest single expenditure on the list is that for "Social Purposes," amounting to 31.7 per cent, or almost a third of the whole budget. The term "Social Purposes" includes such important items as Old Age Pensions, Public Assistance, Unemployed Relief, and Sick and Burial Assistance, each a part of Denmark's comprehensive social program. If we combine the expenditures for "Social Purpose," "Public Education," and "Health" the total amounts to 50.2 per cent of the budget. When such genuine concern is shown for the welfare of all the people as is indicated by this Danish budget, it is no wonder that democracy has assumed real significance and that in this sympathetic environment co-operative housing has been able to flourish.

Varying types of co-operative housing are found in the cities of Copenhagen, Aarhus, Odense, Esbjerg, and in many of the smaller towns of Denmark. Copenhagen contains over 21 per cent of the total population of the entire country, and by far the largest amount of housing has been built in this city.

During the past twenty years nearly a third of Copenhagen's housing has been of the co-operative type. The multi-

family or "flat" type of building accounts for about 70 per cent
of the construction, leaving only 30 per cent in the form of
single dwellings. In recent years practically nothing but multi-
family houses have been built by the co-operative societies,
since these can be provided more economically and supervision is simpler and more effective.

The large Copenhagen societies with one exception retain
ownership of their apartment units, not permitting members
to acquire possession. Only the veteran Workman's Building
Association constructs small houses and allows members to
acquire ownership. The smaller co-operative societies as a rule
sell the dwelling units to their members.

The co-operative societies purchase land for building sites
either from the municipality or from private persons. As described in a previous chapter, the municipality owns considerable ground, enough to meet housing needs for at least
twenty-five years. Formerly the municipality only leased this
land, but today the ground is sold with a stipulation that the
municipality retains the right to buy it back after a number of
years at the price paid, and without taking into account the
value of the buildings placed on it. Due to the availability of
municipally owned land at reasonable prices, privately held
land has not skyrocketed in price; consequently speculation
in this necessary social resource has been restrained. With a
gradual rise in other commodities, the price of land has risen
only about 15 per cent in the last decade.

Co-operative housing societies, because of their social purpose, are allowed tax exemption on their buildings as such.
Taxes on the building sites, however, are based on a system of
assessed valuations made every five years, whereby a certain
percentage rate is established for assessed value and to this is
added a higher percentage rate based on any increase in value
during the last five-year period.

The financing of housing of all types has been greatly simplified by the development of co-operative credit associations. The co-operative and other housing societies obtain their credit largely through land credit associations (*kredit foreninger*), which grant first mortgage loans, and through second mortgage credit associations (*hypothek foreninger*), which, as the name suggests, grant second mortgage loans. These credit organizations are co-operative associations of members seeking loans on the security of their real property. They were started in Denmark as early as 1850, when the Riksdag passed a law permitting their organization under specific regulations, and it is of interest to note they were the first manifestation of the co-operative movement in Denmark. The splendid record of these associations is a testimony to their soundness. Since their start in the middle of the last century, only one credit association has suffered financial difficulties. It was placed under government reorganization and in time was able to pay full principal and interest to its bondholders. As a matter of fact, no bondholder of a credit association has sustained a loss. These credit associations have been considered by the public to be one of the safest forms of investment. Today there are some twelve associations that extend primary credit and nine associations, three of which deal with landed property, extending secondary credit.

Before a construction loan is granted by any of these credit associations, a valuation is made of the building site. As a general rule, a land credit association will grant first mortgage loans up to 45 per cent of the total cost (land, building, and other expenses) expiring in sixty years with interest at 4½ per cent plus a 1 per cent amortization. The second mortgage associations grant loans up to 55 per cent or 60 per cent of the total cost, expiring in forty years with interest at 5 per cent or slightly higher. Since the act of 1933, housing societies have been able to obtain from the state third mortgage loans up to 90 per cent or 95 per cent of the total cost on condition that the municipality guarantee 10 per cent of the loan and that the loan not exceed 40 per cent of the total building costs. In addition, third mortgage loans have been obtained from insurance companies and saving fund societies, which have offered the same terms and conditions as the state, carrying a similar requirement of municipal guarantee of 10 per cent of the loan. The final 5 per cent or 10 per cent equity has been provided by the members in the form of initial deposits.

Admission to membership in a housing society and to occupation of a dwelling unit is available to all those who have sufficient funds to make the initial down payment and whose wage or income allows them to pay the required rent. If dwelling units are not immediately available, numbers are assigned to members as their applications are received and they are allotted accommodations in order as vacancies occur.

The tenant members in many of the co-operative houses are workers, broadly classified, with an average income of about $700 a year. Rents absorb from a quarter to a fifth of this income and are mainly calculated on a square meter basis of space as well as on the number of rooms and conveniences furnished. Rents are also influenced by orientation bearing on exposure and story height. In Copenhagen, for instance, the best exposure is considered to be towards the west, while in the country districts the preferred exposure is east. Ground floor apartments rent for from 5 per cent to 10 per cent less than the floors above. Apartments on the fifth floor of the buildings without elevators rent for about 5 per cent less than the other floors, but in the same type of five-storied building with elevators the fifth floor apartments bring the highest rent. Rents are also affected by the factor of construction costs at the time buildings were erected. As a rule, rents are collected within the first three days of each month by the house-manager of the particular building.

Where a housing society accepts the benefits offered by the

public authorities, i.e., builds on a site purchased from the municipality at a reduced price and uses a third mortgage loan from state funds, the authorities exercise a control over rents, and where the housing embraces a social purpose, directs that the rents be set as low as possible. The proposed rent levels must be approved by the municipality and cannot be raised without consent of the city's representative who is an appointed member of the society's board of directors. Also the accounts are subject to checking by a state official.

When tenants vacate their apartment units they must pay for redecoration and for any repairs that might be deemed necessary by the local representative committee. The costs of this are taken out of the tenant's half-year's rent, paid in advance. No special provisions are made by the housing societies as such to help delinquent or distressed tenants pay their rents. If rents are two or three months in arrears, the tenants are notified in writing, and if no satisfactory response is received they are evicted.

There is a modern office building in Copenhagen that has to go through this life weighted down to the scuppers with the dissonant name of "Axelborg." Perhaps in the Danish tongue it has a pleasant connotation. At any rate, it contained one of the most remarkable pieces of mechanical equipment that I had ever seen. No doubt everyone has at times seen coal, sand, or some other loose material hoisted by means of bucket conveyors attached to a continuously moving chain. Apply this principle to the lifting of people to floors above and you have the elevator system functioning in Axelborg. Merely sets of open-faced compartments, like enlarged phone booths without doors, ceaselessly moving upwards without operators or starter. Due to the fact that one of the large co-operative housing societies occupied offices on the top floor of this five-story building, it was my fate to be a frequent visitor there.

On my first visit I stood appalled in the empty foyer, not a human being in sight, and contemplated my chances of being conveyed to the top floor without bodily injury. To accentuate the terror, a constant clanking noise reverberated through the foyer as the compartments passed the floor. I assumed that of course there must be certain automatic safety devices which would start to operate the moment I made a false move. But what constituted a false move? That was the question. I particularly wanted to ask what would happen to a passenger if, after safely scrambling aboard an ascending compartment, through oversight, absent-mindedness, or paralysis, he should fail to step out when it reached the top floor? Would he go up through the roof and be deposited there gently and unharmed or would he be fed unceremoniously into the gears of the mechanism? In a moment of weakness I was tempted to use a broad stairway on the left but I recalled the strong man's adage, "Live dangerously: when in Axelborg, do as the Axelborgians do." Then, contrari-wise, flashed over my mind the story of the enchanted castle with signs on the doors: "Be bold—enter"; until the last door was reached which bore the sinister sign "Don't be too bold!" The comfortable stairway beckoned; the sinister mechanism challenged. Torn between the two, I decided to take a middle course: I would ride the compartment as far as the fourth floor, bail out if I could and walk up the stairway to the fifth floor. I surmised that if I failed to disembark on the fourth floor I would still have a last chance on the fifth before I went with the compartment through the ceiling and to an inglorious end. It turned out to be a most satisfactory compromise: by gauging the distance accurately and starting the leap off the right foot, I landed in a crouching position in the center of an ascending compartment. Bailing out at the fourth floor was somewhat abrupt and ragged, but it was a great moral victory. Many subsequent trips to the fourth floor improved my technique and I might add that only once was I dragged to the fifth floor as a result of carelessness with loose ends of my clothing—not through any fault of Axelborg's elevator system.

The problem of what happens to passengers failing to make an exit from compartment elevators of this kind was finally solved sometime later in Helsinki, Finland. Riding in an elevator of this type in a new bank building I put the question to my guide. "I'll show you," he replied, and we stayed aboard. Much to my relief our gondola did not turn "bottoms up" as I expected, but kept its upright position as we serenely moved over the top and descended by another shaft. It seems that this elevator system is particularly appropriate for few-story commercial buildings because of its labor-saving feature. I did not make inquiry into the mechanics.

Having conveyed the reader to the fifth floor of the Axelborg building without experiencing the physical discomfort of the author, we find ourselves at the office door of the largest Rochdale co-operative housing society in Denmark. Arbejdernes Andels-Boligforening (the Workmen's Co-operative Housing Society), referred to as A.A.B., belongs to that type of co-operative society which does not allow ownership of property to pass to members nor does it permit members to sell their shares individually. This policy resulted from the unfortunate practice of an earlier period when tenants, being allowed to gradually acquire outright ownership of their dwelling units, sold to speculators, who immediately raised rents, drove out the skilled worker tenants, and reintroduced all the evils which the society had aimed to eliminate.

This society was founded in 1912 with the twofold purpose of operating a co-operative housing society on the Rochdale principles and to provide housing for working people. Today, with over 5,000 members, the society owns some 50 apartment buildings and 150 small single houses, comprising in all about 4,200 dwelling units which accommodate approximately

15,000 persons. In its earlier organization the central membership body had direction over the individual apartment buildings, but the control is now decentralized, with each building unit or apartment house forming an independent branch or "daughter" of the society and managed independently by its elected representatives. Membership is available to reputable persons possessing the necessary 5 per cent equity deposit, which amounts to about one half of the year's rent of the selected apartment. Membership can also be secured by societies or organizations willing to abide by the regulation that all dwelling units must be let to members for their own use, both in the newly built houses and in the older ones when vacancies occur. Another provision states that tenant members cannot be compelled to move out of their dwelling units; on the other hand they may vacate by giving six months notice in advance.

To become a member of the A.A.B. society involves the following procedure: Suppose Carl Jorgensen, a skilled mechanic in Copenhagen, wants to secure a two-room, bath, and kitchen apartment unit in one of the society's "daughter" buildings for his family, which consists of himself, a wife, and one child. Jorgensen has accumulated sufficient savings to meet the required initial deposits. A vacancy has occurred in the particular apartment house which he prefers and he is next on the list for assignment of an apartment. He first takes out a membership share which costs him five kronen, or about $1.15.* He is then required to subscribe for an organization share by obligating himself to pay to the society within the first year of membership 40 kronen, or about $9.20. He will receive 4 per cent yearly interest on this amount and it is returnable to him if and when he withdraws from the society. This organization share gives him the right to take up residence. As a final step, he makes his largest down payment for

* Based on the rate of exchange of 1 kronen = 23 cents.

an apartment share which usually amounts to a half of the first year's rent of the selected apartment. This amount will vary between $70 and $80, depending on the facilities included. He will receive 4 per cent interest on this deposit also, and it will be returned to him upon his withdrawal less the cost of any repairs to the apartment needed as a result of his occupation, and less the cost of redecoration for the next tenant. In addition, a further deduction might occur if the incoming member who takes over Jorgensen's membership pays less for the apartment share than its original purchase price. In other words Jorgensen, by exercising his right of withdrawal, becomes responsible for any decrease in the value of the share. In all cases, the transfer of apartment units and shares takes place only through the organization and not through the individual members. So far, because of the high standing of this society and the constant demand for its accommodations, apartment shares have been transferred at full value, thereby not occasioning any loss to withdrawing members.

Jorgensen is now a full-fledged member of A.A.B. and a tenant in one of their "daughter" buildings. He is in position to benefit materially by the operation of the co-operative principle. He may participate in the "co-operative fund" by paying in to the society a small amount above his monthly rent. If he can afford to do this, he can expect to share in a bonus paid out every five years; $92,000 was distributed from the co-operative fund in 1930 and a like amount followed in 1935. Jorgensen can attend the frequent meetings of the fellow tenants of his building and take part in the annual election of a management committee for the "daughter" building. He and his wife may attend the annual meeting of the entire membership of the society, at which time he will have the opportunity to vote for the members of the central executive committee which will direct the affairs of the society for the next year.

There is no voting by proxy; only members present can vote with one vote for each family regardless of the number of shares held. When the Jorgensens depart homeward after attending the society's annual meeting, they have good reason to hold these comforting thoughts: they have a partnership interest in an active business organization; they are securing their living accommodations at the lowest possible cost because no profits go to outsiders; they have a distinct voice in the management of their own housing affairs; and their interests are protected through joint activity and their home thereby made more secure.

Rents are paid monthly and in advance and are established on a basis which includes interest charges on loans, amortization, taxes, fees, maintenance, and cleaning. Rents also include obsolescence and will be reduced in time as the building grows older.

In the organization of the A.A.B. society, the representatives chosen by the tenants of each building select six members to form a business committee for the central office. As an additional member, a chairman is appointed by the society's executive committee. This business committee employs a salaried business manager and the necessary employed help. Management of the society proper is carried out in this central office from which place the society's general rules and regulations emanate, but management of the independent "daughter" building remains in the hands of the local representatives. Each local management committee selects an individual from among the tenants of the building to act as manager and to run a small office; the committee pays him a modest remuneration or allows him free rent. The local manager collects the rents of tenants and turns them over to a cashier sent out from the central office.

Tenants are responsible for repairs in their own apartments, frequently making the repairs themselves under the supervision of the local management committee. Ordinary exterior repairs are collectively paid for by the tenants of a building. Major repairs or alterations are made by the technical staff of the central office if the local management committee of the building decides to have the work done through this channel —a further instance of the independent character of each building.

Financing of A.A.B.'s new construction work is usually arranged as follows:

	Per Cent
1st mortgage loan from a land credit association	45
2nd mortgage loan from a 2nd mortgage credit association	12
3rd mortgage loan from the state with a part municipal guarantee	38
Tenants' equity (half of year's rent or more)	5

In place of the first and second mortgage loans from the credit associations, a blanket loan is often obtained from savings fund societies. Insurance companies and savings fund societies often provide the third mortgage loans with the municipal guarantee. A co-operative housing society of the social character of A.A.B. pays only 5½ per cent to 6 per cent interest on the third mortgage loans from the state while private builders, although having access to first and second mortgage loans from the credit associations, are required to pay in the neighborhood of 10 per cent for third mortgage loans from private sources. This difference in the interest rate of third mortgage loans reflects itself in the lower rents obtainable in the co-operative housing societies.

In keeping with its name, Workmen's Co-operative Housing Society, the majority of the A.A.B. tenants are listed as workers, using the term broadly. The occupations of the tenant members are as follows:

	Per Cent
Workmen	61
State employees	10
Privately employed	13
Business and professional	9
Miscellaneous	7

To facilitate sound and economical building, the society has branched out into the production of certain building materials. It owns two large brick plants which have been successful as a business undertaking. Further, it owns a plaster of Paris factory and operates a cement plant for the casting of pipes, tiles, bricks, etc. The cement is bought from the Co-operative Cement Works of which A.A.B. is a member. This society is also a member of the Danish Co-operative Bank. It has proven highly beneficial for the different societies to work closely together.

I made a twenty-minute trip by tramcar from the Radhausplatz (City Hall) to see a large housing development of the A.A.B. society located in a section of Copenhagen known as Bronshoj. Danish tramcars, like others I noticed in Scandinavia, prefer seemingly to travel in pairs. There is always a well-appointed lead car pulling around an inferior-looking trailer. Whether this coupling up was for economical reasons or for just affectionate companionship I never was able to discover. I noticed that the inhabitants preferred to jam into the head car on every occasion, leaving the little trailer to trundle along behind only partially occupied. Yet there was no difference in fare to account for this saucy discrimination by the traveling public.

At Bronshoj this society has built four large apartment houses on landscaped ground sloping toward a small artificial lake around which gardens have been planned as part of the project. On the opposite side of the lake, the society had constructed some years ago a number of semidetached two-story cottages without central heat or modern bathrooms. This grouping of the large apartment buildings and cottages forms a branch of the society. A typical building of this group, a red brick, four-story apartment house constructed in 1934, contains modern equipment for the comfortable living of its tenants, who are preponderantly of the working class. Instead of the individual room being heated by stoves as in the municipal buildings, we now find a hot water system with radiators and a central heating plant in the basement. Windows have been fortified with storm sash. Stairway treads and landings have been covered with heavy linoleum. Six-inch wide Swedish pine flooring, with a profusion of knots showing through the thin shellacked finish, extends throughout the apartment units. The kitchens looked much like those in the municipal building except that tiling had been carried around the side walls four and a half feet high. The bathroom in most of the apartments appeared to be in the adolescent stage, not possessing a bathtub but relying on the wide-dispersing shower in the center of the ceiling for bathing purposes. Only the four-room apartment units had bathtubs.

Each group of apartments off a stairway had in the basement its own laundry suite consisting of a washroom, a mangle room, and a drying room. Gas burners heated the washing water on a coin-in-meter system of payment, the cost of an average family's laundry amounting to about thirty cents. Other parts of the basement were used for the storage of family goods in individual latticed compartments and for the storage of bicycles in racks along walls. All heating boilers were together in a large room with coal bunkers adjoining. One engineer ran the plant with a helper for night duty; the former also acted in the capacity of caretaker for the building.

The spacious inside court of this building had many interesting features. All radio aerials were strung to a ring in the center of the court at eave-line height, giving a pleasing order to this otherwise disfiguring appurtenance. Small children were playing in a huge sand box. Near by were metal racks for airing bedding and drying clothes. Numerous racks for bicycles had been provided and, as a thoughtful touch, racks were reserved for visitors' bicycles. A diverting item was an ingenious apparatus for beating carpets. Dirty carpets were dragged by their forelocks into an aerated chamber, sunk a few steps below the level of the court, and spread out on a perforated sheet-metal grate where they received a sound beating. When the housewife turned a switch, an electric intake fan drove air through the louvers at the side and through the grate under the carpet while an exhaust fan sucked out the dust-laden air.

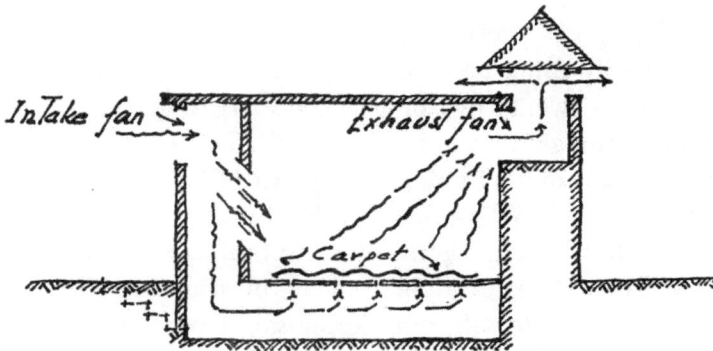

SECTION THRU CARPET BEATING CHAMBER

Another large co-operative housing society is the København Almindelige Boligselskab (the Copenhagen General Housing Society), referred to as K.A.B. This society was organized in 1920 and is both a co-operative association and a joint-stock building company. It owns altogether over seventy-four hundred dwelling units, principally in large multi-family buildings, providing accommodations for some twenty-five thousand persons. In organization it includes: (1) the central or "parent" society, K.A.B., with a number of independent "daughter" societies; (2) the co-operative associations in the Frederiksberg area of Copenhagen, known as Frederiksberg Boligselskab; and (3) the stock building company called Domina. The interrelationship of these associations is somewhat complicated and in a way reminiscent of the intricate organization of an American holding company.

In 1930, K.A.B. absorbed twenty-five self-governing projects of the Frederiksberg Boligselskab (Frederiksberg Housing Society) which had originally been founded by K.A.B. in conjunction with the municipality of Frederiksberg. At the time of this reorganization it was stipulated by the municipality that residents of Frederiksberg (a section of metropolitan Copenhagen which maintained a self-governing status) should be given preference in the occupation of three-quarters of its dwelling units. Other projects have been added to the original twenty-five of Frederiksberg Boligselskab. The Domina company, owned and controlled by K.A.B., administers the affairs of the Frederiksberg association and at the same time acts as a building organization for construction of new housing. K.A.B. also offers complete building service to private individuals, institutions, and organizations. Its advice can be secured on site selection, appraisal of property, building plans, financing, water, gas and sewerage conditions, and other related problems, with fees based on the extent of advice and services rendered.

In order to obtain an apartment in one of the "daughter" houses of K.A.B., a deposit is required of from 5 to 10 per cent of the apartment unit cost (amounting to a half or whole year's rent, depending on cost, location, and other factors). This deposit may be in a lump sum or in installments paid in to the society's Saving Fund Association. Three per cent interest is

COPENHAGEN

One type of small cottage in allotment gardens

STOCKHOLM

A cottage in an allotment garden

These one- and two-room cottages are built for occupancy during the summer months

STOCKHOLM

The cultivation of flowers and vegetables in allotment gardens

STOCKHOLM

A garden colony of a more permanent type than those found in Copenhagen

HELSINKI

Lay-out of a garden colony incorporated in the city plan

allowed, with a stipulation that such deposits cannot be withdrawn in less than two years from time of deposit.

K.A.B.'s housing projects are extensive and widely scattered over Copenhagen. The Ostergaarden apartment house, located in the north section of Copenhagen overlooking a park, deserves mention. Its tenants for the most part are skilled workers, carpenters, plumbers, and others of the building trades. A two-room apartment with kitchen and modern bathroom rents for around $1.75 a month, to which must be added an average monthly charge of $1.85 for heat. For an apartment of this size a deposit of $111.00 is required and is returned to the tenant member upon withdrawal. No interest is allowed on the deposit, this omission being a departure from the practice of the Rochdale type of co-operative housing society.

The Vestervaenget project of this society is located in the southern section of Copenhagen and caters to a somewhat higher income group. A three-room apartment with kitchen and modern bath rents for about $21.00 a month without heat, gas, or electric light. Heat and domestic hot water cost on an average of $2.25 a month. The cost of gas for cooking runs from $.75 to $1.40 a month and electricity from $.50 to $1.40. Apartments fronting on the street have balconies which, by the closing of sash, are converted into alcoves off the living rooms.

Roskildegaarden project of the Frederiksberg branch of K.A.B., built in 1935, shows an increasing trend toward the use of balconies. This decorative and at the same time practical feature is being woven into the so-called "modern" style in some of the more recently built projects, and in those proposed for the future this style is even more pronounced, resulting in a pleasing improvement to the designs of a quarter of a century ago. The chief engineer of the society took me through one of the new apartment houses under construction. Even though this building was intended for low income artisans, I was impressed by the soundness of its construction. Light steel beams, spaced far apart, supported a concrete floor system with a finished wood floor covering of Swedish pine. Rough brick exterior walls were being prepared to receive a stucco plaster coat. Radiators for hot water heating were made of heavy metal plate and hung on the walls with the bottom edge about ten inches from the floor. The type of lathing for the interior walls caught my attention. In place of ordinary wood or metal lath, reeds culled from Danish marshes and wired together were being unrolled from four-foot long bundles and nailed to the studs. I was informed that they made a good key for the plaster and would not rot. The roofs were of Danish fired tile, laid up in the usual manner on wood sheathing.

Laundries were to be provided in the basement, one laundry suite for every ten apartments, in which would be installed the ordinary hand equipment for use without charge. In addition, three electrically equipped laundries were planned where the charge for doing a family wash would amount to about thirty-five cents.

Some people take the most extraordinary precautions to ward off mishaps. I have read that natives in the backwoods of Korea pin bits of brightly colored cloth to tree trunks to attract and hold the attention of evil spirits which might lurk in the neighborhood. Even more civilized persons, those who discourse volubly about gas mileage, remote control, television, and the age of Scotch whisky, often show a certain tendency towards animism. I once knew a political leader, highly respected by his constituents, who always carried a potato in his rear trouser pocket for the purpose of staving off rheumatism. Some years ago I had the rare pleasure of traveling half way across the continent with a hard-boiled executive of a well-known soft drink company who told me confidentially that he always wore his undershirt wrong side out to ward off possible train wrecks. So it goes; each man has his pet superstition, or a number of pets, which influence his daily actions for better or worse. I myself hold fast to a few of the best known superstitions tested by time and accepted in conventional circles. For example, I touch wood or a wood substitute when I catch myself making a boast. I hesitate before walking under sagging ladders. I try to remember to open my umbrella out of doors, not in; and finally, I go out of my way to protect the life of spiders. Much thought and experience have convinced me that a wholesome respect for these minor superstitions removes some of the sharp edges of life and as the golfer says, I am not always playing "out of the rough." So, my practice has been to follow my superstitions rather than my hunches, thereby escaping many of the mishaps that befall less attentive persons. In view of my adherence to this form of moral armament, it was impossible to understand how I could be so abruptly dropped in my tracks on a busy street in Copenhagen.

I had no premonition in the early morning that anything disagreeable would happen to me in the course of that day. I had studiously been observing all my personal superstitions. No uneasy dread disturbed my pleasurable contemplation of another day's inspection of co-operative housing. A trip to see the recently built Kanslergaarden housing project of the A.K.B. society * had been arranged and I carried in my pocket the necessary credentials secured from the society's central office the previous day.

Before I embarked on the tramcar which would weave its slow and tortuous way to the desired housing project, I planned to buy some oranges prescribed by doctor's orders. I had happily found a place where oranges, ordinarily the size

---

* See pp. 117–18 for details of organization.

of jumbo hailstones in Denmark, had actually matured to the magnificent bulk of golf balls. For three little golden nuggets I usually paid twenty-five cents, all of which showed me the possibilities of orange groves in Denmark if the climate could be brought under control. Fruit salesmen of that country have the same professional eminence and position that an art dealer like Duveen has in London. The fruiterer might not be knighted, but the Danish public accord him the same measure of respect. On this regrettable occasion it seems that I insulted the fruiterer by breaking all the orange-buying conventions of Denmark. With true housewifely technique I started to select by a gentle squeeze the oranges desired. This was too much for the orange dispenser. To cast any doubt on his precious fruit was a sacrilege. He turned on me in great indignation and abruptly snatched his cherished oranges out of my hand, muttering Danish invectives, and with significant gestures indicated that our business relations were severed. Gathering up what remained of my shattered self-respect and with one last wistful look at the forbidden fruit, I prepared to cross the wide Vesterbrogaarde to hop a tramcar.

I have previously said that the streets of Copenhagen swarm with bicycles. Stalwart and handsomely uniformed police officers in black helmets and with white long-fingered gloves stand at street intersections and majestically signal hordes of cyclists with all the éclat that would be accorded to motorists. Without the glut of automobiles to snarl the traffic, bicycles hold the stage. If we accept the statement that every third person owns a bicycle in Copenhagen then, on a population basis, it means that there are some two hundred and seventy-five thousand bicycles tinkling their merry way about the city. One soon gets used to their lively presence. My fault was that I began to ignore them altogether. In crossing this wide thoroughfare to reach the plaza in front of the City Hall, my attention became riveted on the graceful outlines of a huge piece of sculpture standing on a pedestal directly ahead. An enormous fairy-tale dragon was being gored to insensibility by an infuriated prize-winning bull, and the sculptor had cleverly developed a fountain idea by letting streams of water spout from the nostrils of the bull and fall as fine spray into a broad basin below. The effect was superb and one's sympathies were entirely with the bull. In constructing the legend behind this stirring combat, it seemed plausible that the farmer owning the bull had unluckily turned up the dragon in his field while ploughing. The dragon promptly devoured his deliverer and the attending team of horses and then ambled his gluttonous way up to the barnyard where the bull was quietly browsing. . . .

I had gotten thus far with this engrossing bit of reconstruction, when suddenly at my elbow came the frantic tinkle of a bicycle bell, pierced by a feminine scream—then the abrupt impact of a wheel against left leg—and we all went down in a heap. The girl cyclist who had dropped me so neatly was on her feet in an instant, apparently unscratched. Her bicycle, which had taken an awkward position across my chest impeded my rising with equal rapidity. We collected the vegetables which had been sprayed from the basket on her handle bars to the street. By this time a few fellow cyclists gathered around. The majestic-looking policeman sauntered over. But there were no harsh words, no taking of names or numbers— in fact, everyone but myself seemed to enjoy the pleasant little break in the daily grind of a Copenhagen cyclist. I hobbled off and boarded the tramcar to continue my journey feeling somewhat shaken and sobered by the untoward events of the morning.

The Kanslergaarden project was built by Arbejdernes Kooperative Byggeforening (Building Worker's Co-operative Association). Founded in 1912 by certain labor organizations, this society owns some twenty-five hundred dwelling units in multi-family apartment houses and single dwellings. The organization, more in the nature of a stock company with limited dividends, retains ownership of its buildings and rents to members in the usual way.

The Kanslergaarden apartment house is a five-story, walk-up building of red brick with red tile roofs and nonfireproof construction. Apartment units are composed of two, three, and four rooms with kitchens and modern bathrooms. Several things were of interest. One outstanding feature was the fact that the architect who designed the building had the courage to live on the premises, occupying an apartment on the fifth floor! In equipment, all the bathrooms, regardless of the size of the apartment units, contained tubs with showers over them; the basement contained both hand and electrically operated laundries, in the latter the work being done by paid laundresses brought in from the outside. And as a minor detail, I liked the restrained design of the doors to the apartment units. The court, open at one end, contained the play facilities in the form of a large round sand box for young children, and a smaller circular space with benches for older people, the latter partially enclosed by a high hedge. Four shops selling dairy products, groceries, candy, and flowers occupied the ground floor of one end of the building. On the whole, this building was exceptionally attractive and complete in its facilities.

The oldest co-operative housing society in Denmark, Arbejdernes Byggeforening (the Workmen's Building Association), was organized by a group of workers in Copenhagen as early as 1865. It has constructed over 1,570 small apartment houses, each containing only two and three dwelling units. Under a lottery system these units have passed into the permanent possession of its members. The small apartment houses have been chiefly built in rows with front and rear gardens. The earlier houses were limited to two stories in height with apart-

ment units consisting of two rooms and a kitchen on each
floor. The later houses of larger size were constructed with a
mansard roof over the second floor, which provided a third
apartment unit.

The ingenious lottery scheme developed by this society to
give the members ownership operates as follows: to provide
working capital each new member is required to contribute
the sum of 2 kroner, or about $.45 a month, for a period of ten
years. At expiration of this period he can either withdraw the
total amount of his contribution plus 4½ per cent accumulated
interest, or he can leave his money with the society and secure
the continuous privilege of participating both in all lotteries
for houses as constructed and in the annual distribution of
dividends. Supplementary to this, a member may participate
in a lottery for a house after six months of membership provided he has paid in 20 kroner, or about $4.60. The winner be-
comes the owner of the house in from twenty-five to thirty
years, depending on the construction cost. During that time
he pays from 50 to 60 kroner, about $11.50 to $14.00, annually in addition to paying the estimated rent of the house,
which rent is always lower than he would have to pay for a
similar dwelling elsewhere.

If a member is lucky enough to win a house in a lottery and
continues to make all of the required payments for the twenty-
five or thirty year period he secures ownership of a building
containing three apartment units. The building costing originally about $3,200 to construct is in this way obtained for a
total payment, exclusive of estimated rent charge, for about
$715.00. From then on he occupies an apartment rent free
and leases out the other two apartments at a good profit. Today this society acts more as a savings fund association than as
a building organization.

In the early years of the twentieth century many pseudo-
co-operative housing societies sprang up in Denmark. Many

of them, organized under the guise of co-operatives for artisan groups, soon developed into profit-making ventures. Speculation became rife, houses were sold and resold at mounting prices, and soon people of means owned them. Because of this and to reaffirm the Rochdale principles the Dansk Havebolig Forening (Danish Garden City Society) was formed in 1912 in Copenhagen. It was stipulated that all houses built should remain the property of the society with the members as tenants. Since one of the main purposes was to further the development of garden suburbs, this society planned and built some 390 houses in the garden suburb of Gröndalsvaenge in Copenhagen. These houses are either single family units or semidetached. They have two rooms, a small hall, and a kitchen on the first floor, and three bedrooms on the second floor. The basement contains rooms for washing and ample storage. Garden space surrounds each house.

The society originally bought the land from the municipality of Copenhagen, to provide for 420 houses in all. The municipality reserved the right to repurchase the land after the year 2000 A.D. at the original sale price, with the city to benefit by any increase in value. A member upon joining the society and occupying a house must pay 20 kroner, or about $4.60 a month, until he has paid in about $140.00 as a deposit. He also pays his rent charge which may run from $10.25 to $13.50 a month depending on the size of the house. Included in the rent payments is amortization of the mortgage loan which serves to reduce the rent gradually. When a member moves, thereby losing his membership in the society, the $140.00 deposit is returned to him plus the amount he has contributed toward the amortization of the mortgage loan of the property. In addition he is compensated for improvements made to the house and grounds.

One of the more recently organized co-operative housing societies is the Forenigen Social Boligleggere (the Building

Stock Company), established in 1933 and representing a form of housing society akin to the half-public and half-private societies found in the other Scandinavian countries. Promoted with the assistance of the municipality of Copenhagen, this society cannot change its by-laws and regulations without the approval of the city and the Minister of Interior, nor can it secure loans without the consent of the city which has a major control over it. Its purpose is to build small apartment units in Copenhagen and near-by towns, utilizing both state and municipal aid. The administration is lodged in the central organization and each building enterprise constitutes an independent branch or "daughter" society. All surplus earnings of the branches are paid to the central organization and put into a reserve fund used to meet any losses occurring in the branches and to finance new construction of housing. The municipality of Copenhagen guarantees all obligations of the society, and in turn it is stipulated that the society's property becomes the city's possession in the year 1960. In reality, this society takes on the character of a municipal housing agency.

In addition to the larger housing societies, there are a number of smaller organizations throughout the country which build both for members and outsiders. Also, there are scattered through Denmark numerous share companies called *"byggeaklieselskaber,"* which are private groups composed of builders, architects, and lawyers organized to promote building enterprises and distribute shares according to individual contribution. While most of these companies have little or no social character they have played a prominent part in private building activity and are mentioned for general interest.

The extent of co-operative housing in Denmark is a notable achievement. The question naturally arises: Why have the Danes so wholeheartedly embraced the principles of co-operation? An answer comes from the pen of the eminent Danish scholar, Carl Gad, Rector of the Ingrid Jespersen

School in Copenhagen. In drawing a comparison between the earliest Danish poetry and the corresponding poetry of Norway and Iceland (practically nothing remaining of the Swedish literature of that time), he shows that Norwegian and Icelandic poetry concerns mostly man's relation to the supernatural powers, while in Danish poetry the central feature is man's life among his fellow men. He admits that the psychology of the Norwegian-Icelandic poetry is incontestably more profound, but that in the Danish, the figures are more imposing by virtue of their unity and harmony. He ends by drawing this superb characterization:

"One trait of these heroes, a trait that has in fact descended in the Danish character, is the ponderous calm and tenacity of purpose which marks them. The taciturn Uffe, whose indolence is only on the surface, who wakes up to deeds of daring at the right moment; Rolf Krake, the favourite king of the legends, who exalts patience as the leading virtue; the grizzled Starkad, in Inggjald's lay, who is greeted with the mockery of the king's men but is able to revive the slumbering heroism of the monarch; and Hamlet, who, under the cloak of his simulated madness, works purposefully towards his vengeance; the same primordial character marks them all: they are men who are never precipitous and never comport themselves with fiery passion, but surely and steadily achieve what they consider to be their aim, without extravagance of word or gesture." *

SWEDEN

Traveling from Denmark to Sweden, let us loiter for a moment at Elsinore, a point on Danish soil almost within hailing distance of the town of Helsingborg on the Swedish coast. The name Elsinore has such a melodious ring that I think of

---

* In *Denmark, a Collection of Monographs* (Copenhagen, C. A. Reitzel's Publishing Co., 1935).

it as belonging to the poetry of Coleridge. He might have awakened from his slumber and written, "In *Elsinore* did Kubla Khan a stately pleasure dome decree. . . ." And of course the spell of Hamlet has long lent enchantment to the name. Even though we know that the life of the legendary prince was extinguished a thousand years before the celebrated Kronborg castle was built, yet the atmosphere seems to be charged with realism. On the castle's terrace (or "landing" as noted in the play) overlooking the sea we walk in the footsteps of Hamlet. We vision the meeting with his father's ghost and relive the scene.

But Kronborg has more than legend to support its fame. Erected in the latter part of the sixteenth century, it was to be a symbol of Denmark's supremacy in the Baltic, the sentinel standing guard at the entrance to the sound. For almost three hundred years the Danes collected dues from all ships sailing through the sound, and Elsinore grew prosperous. The exacting of tolls was abandoned in 1857, and today Kronborg stands divested of all military power—a fortress turned into a maritime museum with a meeting place in its great Knight's Hall for assemblies of Swedes and Danes in peaceful conference.

Across this narrow two-mile stretch of water separating Denmark and Sweden has flowed an interchange of ideas. In certain respects Denmark has been the laboratory for social experiments. The folk high school movement trekked northward from Denmark into Sweden, Norway, and Finland. While Sweden received its direct impulse for establishing co-operatives from England, the earlier accomplishments along co-operative lines in Danish agriculture no doubt paved the way for Swedish adoption. And the early development of co-operative housing in Denmark had its influence on Sweden.

Co-operative housing in Sweden before the World War

was limited to small independent undertakings composed of single dwellings and two-apartment unit houses. During the war, due to the housing shortage, pseudo-co-operative housing grew rapidly, especially in Stockholm. These early organizations were on the order of commercial ventures with the profit motive emphasized. Dwellings were sold to property owners, speculation flourished; in consequence, the social purpose suffered. However, certain good resulted from these early co-operative forms. They welded groups together, introducing some spirit of co-operation; they contributed substantially toward relieving the housing shortage; and lastly, they laid the groundwork for the acceptance of more social forms of co-operative housing.

In 1916, in order to remove the profit motive feature, reform principles were established whereby co-operative societies retained ownership of their houses or dwelling units and replaced the old idea of purchase by members with the permanent right of occupancy of quarters. The first important co-operative society of this type, established in Stockholm in 1916, was the Stockholms Kooperative Bostadsforening (The Co-operative Housing Society of Stockholm) initiated by the Central Union of Social Labor and organized with the assistance of the municipality. This society followed the principle that houses should not be purchased but should be built for its members; that members would be given permanent right of occupancy and that their initial deposit would be refunded to them when they vacated. S.K.B.'s form of organization provided a model for other co-operative housing societies of this kind. It has built over 1,785 dwelling units in Stockholm and has some 2,000 members.

All told, about twenty thousand members occupy accommodations in co-operative housing societies in Stockholm. These societies generally fall into two classifications; they are either "right of occupancy associations," which let out their dwelling units with permanent right of occupancy (according to the law of 1930, tenants and their dependants may not be excluded from their quarters if certain conditions are fulfilled), or "renting associations," which rent out their dwelling units. In both cases membership is required. The initial or membership fee varies from about $12 to $50, and the second down payment at time of occupation of dwelling unit amounts usually to 10 per cent of the cost value of the dwelling unit, proportionate to the cost of the whole building. Interest is paid on this deposit.

Except for certain organizations, the co-operative housing societies and building associations are of a private character. This is a more or less accepted status despite the fact that the societies have received, in the past, government aid in the form of state loans, municipal loans, cheap land sites acquired from the municipalities, and have municipal officers sitting on their boards and checking accounts.

Where municipalities owned the land and would only rent it (as prevalent in the suburbs of Stockholm, for instance), difficulties were encountered in securing mortgages from private credit organizations. Therefore some municipalities organized special credit institutions, usually in the form of joint-stock companies controlled by the municipalities. Stockholm organized Aktiebolget Stockholms Tomtrattskassa with the city as the largest stockholder. This organization has the right to issue bonds which are guaranteed by the municipality. Interest charges are slightly higher than they would be in the case of an applicant owning the site and securing a loan from a private credit source.

Very few visitors to Stockholm escape hearing about the wonders of Hyresgasternas Sparkasse och Byggnadsforening (The Tenants' Savings Bank and Building Society), better known as H.S.B. Its aims and achievements have been heralded from penthouse and roof garden. It is the largest co-operative housing society in Sweden. It operates branches in over sixty cities, towns, and communities, and is constantly exploring new fields. In Stockholm alone this society has built over ten thousand dwelling units and boasts of over eleven thousand five hundred members. It has organized a National Union, composed of all its societies, and issues bonds to its members to secure working capital. H.S.B. offers a wide choice of accommodations at different price levels. Organized as late as 1923, it has experienced a phenomenal growth, attested by the figures showing that the assessed valuation of all its buildings exceeds $35,000,000.

H.S.B. is as complicated in its make-up as Scotch haggis. In the first place, a head or "parent" society exists in each city or municipality where H.S.B. has been established. The chief purpose of this "parent" society is to initiate and construct the building enterprises, and to act as the executive body in the locality. Next, each building erected becomes a subsidiary society, holding a kind of dual relationship with the "parent" society: the subsidiary society exercises a degree of self-management, but at the same time is allied to the "parent" organization to which it fulfils certain financial obligations and is subject to a measure of administrative control. And finally, there is the National Union of H.S.B., a federated body of all the "parent" societies in Sweden. This union conducts a savings bank through the local "parent" organizations, allowing H.S.B. members to draw 3½ per cent interest on deposits with the right of withdrawal upon notice. Deposits are used as both primary and secondary credit for new construction and move from one project to another. Further, the union assists the local societies in different municipalities by legal counsel, advice on financing, preparation of drawings, drafting of forms and budgets, and many other activities related to construction and management of projects.

In Stockholm, the general financial plan of the society proposes to repay membership deposits after twenty or twenty-five years. An amount equal to the deposits of the members is lent by the "parent" society to the subsidiary society as soon as the building has been completed, and the subsidiary society is obliged to amortize this loan within twenty or, in the case of certain buildings, twenty-five years. The subsidiary society collects the money required for such amortization from the tenants in the form of annuities included in the monthly payments. In addition, a fee of 2½ per cent of the assessed valuation of the real estate is payable in twenty years, the revenues of which are added to the reserve fund of the "parent" societies.

In other H.S.B. societies in Sweden the creation of capital is arranged in a different manner, and the deposits of members are not repaid. The financing of a housing project is managed in this way: A first mortgage loan up to 60 per cent of construction cost is obtained from a bank. Secondary credit up to about 90 per cent or 95 per cent of the construction cost is covered by the savings bank deposits and the working capital of the National Union and parent societies. The final 5 per cent or 10 per cent, as the case may be, is obtained from initial deposits of the members. A refinancing takes place after construction of the building. State and municipal loans are obtained occasionally.

H.S.B. offers four types of housing: A, B, C, and D. The A and B types are co-operative. In A type, the applicant for an apartment unit must take out a membership share costing about $13 and deposit 10 per cent of the cost value of the apartment unit. For the B type, the same membership fee is required plus a deposit of 5 per cent of the value of the apartment unit. The C type is intended for tenants who cannot afford to pay any deposit. In this case the municipality, having aided by making loans and furnishing building sites at reduced cost because of the social purpose, exercises a certain control over rents and selection of tenants. The D type is intended for poor families with many children. Here H.S.B. acts as a public utility housing agency for the city. The state provides loan funds for second mortgages from 50 per cent to 95 per cent of the assessed value of the buildings and H.S.B. advances the remaining 5 per cent equity. This D type of quasi-private housing, substantially aided by the government, has previously been described in the chapter, "Municipal Housing."

The total number of dwelling units owned by H.S.B. are divided as follows: 20 per cent, single rooms with kitchenette; 33 per cent, one room and kitchen; 30 per cent, two rooms and kitchenette; and 10 per cent, two rooms and kitchen. In the D type for the poorer families, three to four bedrooms with kitchen, living room, and dining room units are provided; these constitute part of the remaining 7 per cent.

Not many blocks from the picturesque Town Hall of Stockholm stands a group of apartment buildings belonging to H.S.B. Literally carved out of the rocky ascending ground, these eight-story buildings of the A type represent the most up-to-date developments in Swedish apartment house planning. With central heat plants in their basements, elevators, roof gardens, and all the latest mechanical and sanitary equipment, they offer to their tenants more amenities than could be found in many "luxury flats" of private enterprise. Superimposed balconies not only provide direct access to sun and air for the dwellers, but also add to the attractiveness of design.

The social and recreational features offered by H.S.B. to its membership account in no small measure for its success in the housing field. The society appears to be blazing a trail in supplying services for its members which are likely to have a salutary effect on other organizations. The facilities offered by H.S.B. include day nurseries where mothers can leave their children for the day if they are engaged in outside employment. There are kindergartens, places equipped for joinery and gymnastics, and outdoor playgrounds. The attendance of one child at kindergarten costs about fifteen cents a day, and twenty-five cents for two children. In 1935 H.S.B. established a Children's Hotel to care for sick children or to board those whose parents were temporarily absent or undergoing an emergency, the cost for care being fifty cents a day for each child. H.S.B. has also established a summer resort at Årsta on the Swedish coast, where members can either buy summer cottages at moderate cost or rent them for a vacation period. Lectures and training courses are conducted. In addition, H.S.B. arranges for its members to take out life insurance through the insurance company of the Swedish consumers' co-operative society whereby wives, children, and the home are insured against the death of the family head. Further, a special fund has been set up to repurchase apartments of members who desire to dispose of them by reason of unemployment or other causes. Finally H.S.B. has in its organization a department devoted to the examination and testing of new building materials and methods of construction. Records show that over 60 per cent of the occupants of H.S.B. housing fall into the broad classification of workers; some 10 per cent are minor officials in public and private service; another 24 per cent are clerks in stores; and the remaining 6 per cent are professional persons, engineers, teachers, and others.

In addition to the two large co-operative societies, S.K.B. and H.S.B., there are, according to the directory, some five hundred smaller housing societies of various types. A large number of these are members of the Central Association of Housing Societies. Organized in 1921 with two hundred members and composed of co-operative housing associations and private individuals owning property in Sweden, this central association serves its membership in a number of beneficial ways. The most important services are: establishing contact with the public authorities and watching legislation affecting housing matters; furnishing free legal advice; providing information for income tax returns; and giving information about the securing of loans, bookkeeping, auditing, and the like.

While philanthropic housing in Stockholm has been comparatively limited in the actual amount of housing accommodations provided, its importance in earlier times was substantial. As a social agency, practically alone in the housing field, it met a part of the housing need of the low income group. As far back as the middle of the last century a society was formed by public subscription called "The Fund for Dwellings for Laborers" to commemorate an event which in description quaintly ignores feminine collaboration: "The King's happy recovery of his health coupled with the event of the birth of His Royal Highness the Hereditary Prince, so joyous to the nation." The purpose of this society was to erect sound and inexpensive dwellings for laborers, and it has built some 558 apartment units which accommodate approximately 2,-170 persons. Units of one room and kitchen rent for about $132 a year without heat and $213 with heat.

A total of approximately eight thousand dwelling units in Stockholm have been provided by the various philanthropic societies. Over two thirds of these are occupied by persons listed as old people, single women, and the like. Generally speaking, these societies have been founded with some form of municipal aid, but with a few exceptions they retain a strictly private status. During the past few years there has been but a small amount of philanthropic housing constructed.

As is usual elsewhere, philanthropic housing societies in Stockholm are organized either as limited dividend companies or as foundations. In the former category they are subject to certain governmental regulations, while in the latter they are permitted wider powers, but remain under the control of the governor general. The buildings erected are for the most part multi-family, not single or semidetached, and all accommodations are rented rather than sold. A brief summary of some of the more important societies follows:

THE WILHELM GOVENI MINNE FOUNDATION. Established in 1903 for persons of small means belonging to the laboring class; gives preference to needy widows and minors. It has built 374 apartment units, housing approximately 1,370 persons. The average annual rent for an apartment of one room and kitchen is $96.20 without central heat or $149.50 with central heat.

BRUZELLI DONATION FUND. Established in 1906; owns 276 apartment units, accommodating 500 tenants. THE B. A. DANELII DONATION FUND, established in 1909; owns 350 apartment units accommodating 660 tenants. Both of these funds are intended for young women workers. They are administered by the Financial Commission of the municipality of Stockholm.

MAGNA SUNNERDAHL DONATIONS. Created in 1914 and 1922 for the purpose of providing sound and inexpensive housing for reputable persons of small means, preferably workers' families with many children, especially from the vicinity of Sodermalm.

HOMES FOR OLD PEOPLE. Established in 1927 in various parishes. For people who have seen better days and can no longer afford to pay normal rents.

THE ST. ERIK BUILDING SHARE COMPANY. This association is one of the oldest of the limited dividend companies. It was founded in 1875 to provide suitable and sound homes for the poorer population of Stockholm and owns some 402 apartment units providing accommodations for approximately 600 persons. Annual rents for one room and kitchen vary between $91 and $117. Dividends are limited to 6 per cent.

STOCKHOLM'S HOMES FOR WORKERS, INC. For persons with small means, somewhat similar to Octavia Hill in London. A share-holding company with a limited dividend of 4 per cent. The number of tenants in 1933 was 1,940 persons in 9 houses with a total of 588 apartment units. Average annual rent for apartments of one room and kitchen amounted to $109 without central heat or $202 with central heat.

THE HOLMIA HOUSING SHARE COMPANY. Formed in 1898 as a limited dividend company to provide suitable and cheap living quarters for workers in Stockholm. Dividends are limited to 4 per cent. It owns 675 apartment units accommodating some 2,000 persons at an average rent of $117 for one room and kitchen, without central heat.

CHEAP LIVING QUARTERS, INC. Founded in 1898. It is a small, 4 per cent limited dividend organization taking care of some 221 persons in three multi-family houses, renting for approximately $45 a year for a single room with cook stove, and $91 a year for a one room and kitchen unit.

VANADISLUNDEN HOUSING SHARE COMPANY. Founded in 1903 for persons of small means, preferably workers. This is another limited dividend organization owning 119 apartment units, occupied by 300 persons. The average rent amounts to $98 a year for one room and kitchen, without central heat.

THE BLOMSTERGÅRDEN SHARE COMPANY. Organized in 1924 and now the largest of the philanthropic housing societies. It owns 695 apartment units, occupied by approximately 995 persons. The average yearly rent amounts to about $213 for one room and kitchen with central heat. It is for aged and infirm persons of small means who are residents of Stockholm.

A young engineer and his companion whisked me out by motor from my hotel in Stockholm to see a new housing project for industrial workers, known as Hjorthagen, located in the east end of the city. The first units had been built in 1935–1936 to house employees of the Vartan Gas Works, a public utility corporation of Stockholm. It was unique in that the workers themselves had promoted it. I turned to the engineer and asked the name of the man who conceived the idea. He

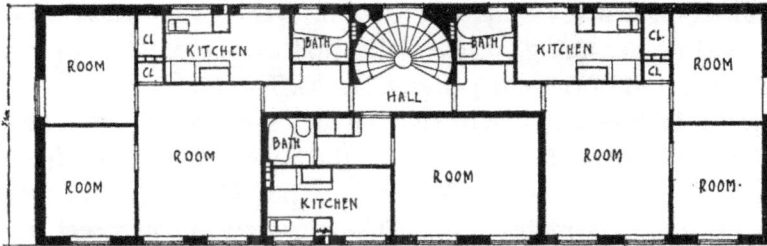

A Hjorthagen Floor Plan

replied quickly, "The man sitting beside you. He is one of the workers in the utility company and it was through his tireless efforts that the project was built. He is now its manager. He doesn't speak English." Of the many occasions when I regretted my inability to converse in Swedish, this seemed the most unfortunate. One glance at Mr. Lindblad's honest ruddy face and bright kindly eyes assured me that he had a sympathetic understanding of his fellow worker's needs, and I should like to have secured from him in his own words the story of his housing project.

The group of three-story buildings occupy a site overlooking a large public park. They are arranged in long rows separated by open spaces not yet landscaped to any degree. The effect of whitish-gray finish on brick walls is relieved by bands of buff color around the entrances to apartment units. The gently inclined lean-to roofs add to the simplicity of design.

Circular steel pressed staircases with cement treads lead to the upper floors. Doors to apartments are finished in natural birch laid out in squares divided by thin wood strips.

The buildings were constructed on an economical principle: light aerated bricks, made from a mixture of clay and sawdust, had been used in the outside walls, and because of the limited strength of these bricks the weight of the floors rested on heavier transverse bearing walls, the outside walls therefore becoming curtain walls. Nonbearing partitions were constructed of two-inch cinder blocks. The prefabricated materials included the stairways, kitchen equipment, and casement windows. As quite usual, the building site had been leased from the city for a sixty-year period at a cost of fifty cents a square meter a year. The city had put in street improvements, including such services as water, gas, electricity, and sewerage.

Of the 478 apartment units constructed, the most popular type is the two-room, kitchen, and bath unit. Kitchens are equipped with rustless steel sinks and small gas stoves, but without mechanical refrigeration. Rent for an apartment of this type amounts to about $226 a year. A smaller one-room, kitchen, and bath apartment rents for around $200, while the rent of three-room apartments runs as high as $266 a year. As the worker's average annual wage in the Vartan plant ranged from $910 to $1,040, it can be seen that the ratio of rent to income is proper. The ownership of apartment units remains in the hands of the housing society, and tenant members rent the apartments in the usual manner. To secure accommodations in this housing the head of a family deposits about $250 and on this amount he receives 6 per cent yearly interest.

The financing of the project was accomplished as follows: a first mortgage of 40 per cent of the cost of the project at 3.6 per cent interest was obtained from a large life insurance company; a second mortgage up to 75 per cent of the project at 3.6 per cent interest was secured; and the third mortgage up to 90 per cent came from a state loan at 7½ per cent interest, which included amortization in twenty years. The remaining 10 per cent represented deposits of workers.

Modern equipment relieves laundry drudgery for the tenants; two kinds of electrical washers have been installed, one kind for light washing and another for the heavy pieces. There are electrical wringers and drying rooms with mechanically warmed air dryers; ironing rooms with electric hand irons and mechanical mangles for large pieces. A charge of seventy-five cents a day is made for the use of all the equipment.

Housing at Kvarnholmen for the employees of the Three

Single House Plan at Kvarnholmen

Crown flour mill of Kooperativa Förbundet (the Wholesale Society and Union of Consumers' Co-operative Societies), briefly referred to as K.F., is rightfully one of the showplaces of Stockholm. Situated on a beautiful island in the harbor within sight of the city, this project is another fine example of modern housing for industrial workers. K.F., the consumers co-operative wholesale society for Sweden, in addition to the operation of the Three Crown flour mill, is engaged in numerous manufacturing activities, including the production of margarine, vegetable oil, cattle food-cakes, rubber goods, shoes, electric bulbs, and many other essential commodities.

K.F. purchased Kvarnholmen Island for its mill and housing outright from the city. Single houses were erected in 1929 and the apartment multi-family buildings in 1934 and later. The single houses, thirty altogether, have been placed in ascending rows on the hillside so that each house retains the advantage of an unobstructed view over water. Each contains one large room and a smaller one, a kitchen and bath, with a basement under the front part of the house and a terrace. There is also an attractive slip of a garden on the southern exposure for each of the houses. Rents are approximately $300 a year, which includes hot water and heat from a central plant. Gas and electricity are furnished at additional cost.

The multi-family buildings containing apartment units are located on the crest of the hill and command a magnificent view over the harbor. Typical two-room, kitchen, and lavatory apartments with heat rent for about $175 a year, and apartment units located at the ends of the buildings with larger rooms and bath rent for about $200 a year. The renting of accommodations in this housing absorbs approximately one fifth of the tenants' income. The single houses, renting for about 30 per cent more than the apartment units in the flats, are occupied by the higher paid employees. Management of the housing is in the hands of K.F. and is directed from its central office. Tenants are employees in the flour mill and accommodations are rented in the usual manner. Facilities include laundries with electrical equipment available without charge. A Konsum, the Swedish co-operative grocery store, is centrally located. Bus service takes the children to the nearest schools on the mainland, about twenty minutes away.

Viewing this admirable industrial project, the wooded island, the modern flour mill buildings at the water's edge, the sound and attractive housing for the employees, the tenants' assembly hall for dramatic activities, study groups, lectures, entertainments, and what not, the spacious playgrounds for the children, and the winding walks through pine and spruce greenery—all of this made me recall with something of a shudder a too-familiar factory scene in an industrial town in western Pennsylvania. Just outside the high grilled fence enclosing a well-appointed factory building stood a gaunt row of soot-begrimed frame shacks, mere shells of buildings without sanitary facilities, and which under the lowest standards could hardly have been relegated to animals. Not a blade of grass to cover the stark nakedness of flat baked ground, not a shrub or bush to relieve the surrounding dreariness, not a tree to cast a shadow and give relief from the blistering rays of a July sun. Yet in these hovels workers and their families eked out their dismal existence. The imposing industrial plant representing enterprise and commercial progress and the dilapidated hovels representing social disintegration! The contrast was absurd—a blind spot in the evolutionary process. Could reasoning man be so stupid as to think there is no connection between how well a man works and how terribly a man lives? Or do many employers look upon their workers only as "animals with motion but with little decision"? Men living in hovels become animals with little decision and worse.

Society has long known that the health and disposition of workers have a direct bearing on their working ability. Over half a century ago Lord Palmerston, in his last illness, wrote to Gladstone: "If men were mere machines which would regularly do a given quantity of work in a given time like a steam engine, such calculation would be unanswerably decisive, but in considering such matters we ought to bear in mind that men are moral and intellectual agents, and that the work performed by them in a given time depends much on the cheerfulness and good-will with which it is done, and that both cheerfulness and good-will very much depend upon the belief that those who superintend and direct have some sympathy for the employed."

Hjorthagen and Kvarnholmen projects represent two types of industrial housing for workers. In the first case, to obtain suitable housing the employees of the Vartan Gas Works were helped to help themselves by legitimate financing from both public and private sources. In the second case, a large co-operative society, acting as an employer interested in the welfare of its employees, constructed the housing. Both methods are applicable in a free society.

The municipality of Gothenburg has greatly encouraged co-operative construction by extending direct subsidies and granting substantial loans. Co-operative housing started as early as 1872 with the organization of the Workmen's Building Society, modeled after the A.A.B. society in Copenhagen. Some twenty-four small apartment houses were built, composed of three apartment units to a house. Each unit was made up of one room, a kitchen, a *spisrum*, and a *bryagtuga*, the latter a room which today is used as a laundry. The society discontinued business in 1898.

One of the most active branches of the H.S.B. society operates in Gothenburg where it is responsible for most of the construction in the local housing field. Since 1926 it has been building an average of two hundred dwelling units a year.

The city has aided the society by granting second and third mortgage loans up to 90 per cent of the total cost. Formerly the society built almost exclusively one-room and kitchen dwelling units, but an extra room has been added to the planning within recent years. A unit comprising one large room and a smaller room with kitchen and bath, a total floor area of some 462 square feet, rents for about $215 a year and requires an initial down payment of $286. In some of the later buildings these rents have been slightly lowered due to the adoption of smaller kitchens, which reduced floor space. H.S.B. has also erected a substantial number of two- and three-apartment unit houses of larger floor area, which rent for a larger sum.

Co-operative housing for industrial workers has played an important part in Gothenburg housing, having raised housing standards and been of substantial aid to public welfare. Among the co-operative organizations established during the World War housing shortage is the Gamlestaden Factories' Share Company which was organized for the workers with financial aid from the owners of the factories. Another in the same category is the Mechanical Factories' Share Company. These two organizations produced altogether 209 dwelling units for their workers. Also in the field of housing built by employers for their workers is that known as the Share Company of the Swedish Ball-Bearing Factories, which, with some similar companies, has provided a total of six hundred dwelling units. Finally, to include the most important contributions in housing for the less well-to-do of this city, mention should be made of the half-public and half-private share companies called Framtiden and Nutiden, the former receiving the greater part of its share capital from the city and the latter a smaller amount. Together these stock societies have built houses containing over 572 apartment units occupied by low income families with many children.

A number of philanthropic housing societies exist in Gothenburg for the purpose of providing quarters for the low income groups. Among the most prominent of these is the Robert Dickson Foundation which dates back in organization to 1859, and owns some 550 dwelling units, its rents being 30 per cent below the market rate. Another similar organization is the Emily Dickson Foundation, which built housing for low income families with many children. There is also the Seamen's Society, which rents its dwelling units to retired officers and sailors of the merchant marine.

Most of the co-operative organizations in the city of Malmö were founded after 1920, and their lively activities have been responsible for a substantial amount of the housing erected. H.S.B. is the largest society, having erected in the period 1925–1934 some sixteen houses containing nearly seven hundred apartment units. At the end of 1933 there were seventy-one co-operatively managed houses containing about twenty-five hundred apartment units. Malmö, like other Swedish municipalities, is steadily adding to the membership in co-operative housing enterprises.

FINLAND

"Yes, the Finns are a fine people. They pay their debts," warmly declared a member of our group as we chatted together at one of those light buffet luncheons deemed so indispensable to the success of an American housing conference. We had been discussing the social progress of the Baltic Sea folk, and the speaker, an old business acquaintance, spontaneously added his praise. But as he caught my eye, I noticed a repentant look, as much to say, "Oh-oh, I should never have said that!" I suspected the reason for his regret. A few minutes later we were seated beside each other waiting for the introductory remarks of the chairman. Suddenly he turned to me and in a low voice filled with earnestness said, "I want you to know I haven't forgotten about that money I owe you. I am going to pay it." "Praise to the Finns," I thought. "That little slip you made about paying their debts is going to cost you money!" I replied, "That's fine, George, I'm glad to hear you say it. I could use the money nicely at this time." We lapsed into silence and in a few moments the chairman started his introductory remarks. The next day, following up the lead, I decided to pen a gentle little reminder and wrote, "Dear George, Regarding our conversation yesterday, I thought your remark about the Finns' paying their debts was most appropriate and I have taken to heart your sincere expression of good faith and timely assurance that the outstanding indebtedness would be cleared up. You have put me in a mood of cheerful expectancy which I feel is but a short and sweet prelude to a complete settlement. I might add, however, that in case a full payment at this time might incommode you, I would suggest monthly installment payments over a year's time. It was a distinct pleasure seeing you yesterday. . . ." A month rolled by with no answer to either support or crush my cheerful expectancy. Then by chance I met the champion of Finnish honor on the street. He pulled out a check from his pocketbook and with somewhat of a flourish handed it to me saying, "I have been waiting to give you this check. I want to clean up the account by monthly payments." I glanced at the check, the first installment, and was not staggered by its amount, but it was something nevertheless, and my hopes revived. But the story ends here—no more payments followed. Evidently the strain was too much for the bank account. Even so, I am indebted to the Finnish government whose honor and integrity inspired one small payment on an overdue account. And who knows, others may have benefited in the same way!

Writing to a friend after the first few days in Helsinki, I

commented, "This country, in the flush of youth, is beginning to do real creative work along sensitive lines. New patterns are being made, new forms are being moulded. The Finns are mindful of Goethe's comment that 'there is nothing more fearful than *imagination* without *taste*,' so they combine the two. Not all patterns, not all forms have this merit, but enough to engender the impression. . . . Here is an atmosphere of vigor, sincerity and beauty."

One does not have to look for expressions of vigor only on the sports field, though it happens that the Finns have made athletic records which have amazed the world. Vigor is expressed in their walk—an easy motion of the hips, a swinging of the legs, and a planting of the feet that brings a rhythmic glide which sweeps the body forward at an uncommonly swift pace. Not the staccato jauntiness of the Britisher's walk, but the graceful movement of the tiger—and my cat. Of course not all Finnish people show this characteristic, for there are the lame, the halt, the blind, and other exceptions.

Nor does one look for aesthetic values only in picture galleries or in the façades of buildings. Beauty can be seen in the shop windows and stores along the street; silver, metal, and wood-craft shops in Helsinki display modern pieces which are fresh and crisp in their design and at the same time possess good taste; the shapes and colors of pottery show the imprint of imaginative craftsmen; handwoven fabrics exemplify the spirit of the new creative Finland. These expressions of craftsmanship go far to demonstrate the grounded artistry of the people and provide a foundation upon which the larger forms can be built. While realizing that comparisons are sometimes odious because they seem to insult the pride rather than disclose truth, I wonder what aesthetic value archaeologists of some distant age will place upon the unearthed products of today's gift shops and roadside pottery stands scattered over our American countryside. Will they be as eager to ascertain the names of the craftsmen as those who, in this generation, seek to identify the designers of ancient Greek vases? I fear they will weary of indiscriminate digging and will concentrate their efforts on the search for Indian relics. Pottery by "Marie," fabrics and jewelry of the Navahoes and other western tribes may lead them to the conclusion that only Indians, in an age of industrialism, had time and talent to devote to craftsmanship.

Turning to the larger art forms, the Parliament House in Helsinki deserves special praise because of its dignified beauty. Built of native pink granite and following a rather liberal conception of the classical style, it stands as a fitting tribute to the skill and genius of its designer, Professor J. S. Siren. The imposing façade is simplicity itself: a great flight of monumental steps, extending almost the entire length of the building, sweeps up to the stately screen of towering Corinthian columns which supports a geometrically decorated entablature. The walls of the long State Hall, inside, are painted a pale yellow shade, the floor is inlaid with native Lolmarden and Calacata marble, and a beamed ceiling is finished in soft green and gray tones. In the circular Hall of Session where Parliament meets and records its votes electrically, grayish-green walls provide a contrasting background for the gilt-capped columns which encircle the hall and support the rotunda. Gilded figures have been placed in the wall behind the speaker's desk, each symbolizing a phase of life; for instance, in the central niche is the figure of a woman with a child in her arms. In beauty and interest, no detail of this building has been neglected.

Other fine architectural examples of this new republic include the well-known Helsinki railroad station designed by Eliel Saarinen, the beautiful and impressive interior of the

Helsinki Crematorium, the Workmen's Institute Building, the National Public School, and the Army Hospital in Viipuri with its interesting main entrance.

It has been said, "Look only once to see beautifully. Look twice to see accurately." We have looked once and found beauty. If we look twice to ascertain what social expression may lie in the field of housing, we do not experience the same stimulation. Co-operative housing, so active in other Scandinavian countries, remains underdeveloped in Finland. This seems strange in view of the fact that Finland has so readily applied co-operation in other fields. The reason it has occupied such a minor position is due to the popularity of "the joint-stock lodging society," a profit-motivated form of housing peculiar to this country.

After Finland's War of Independence, rents increased greatly. This brought an increase in the living cost of wage earners and at the same time induced a revival of the building industry. Between the years 1920 and 1926 the state advanced large credits in the form of emergency grants and repayable loans, both based on the stipulation that the municipalities make substantial contributions. These state funds were utilized by municipally organized housing companies, building societies, and private individuals, and accounted for some 40 per cent of the construction work done during this period. In 1927 this program was abandoned and in its place the government set up a "State Fund for Popular Dwellings," which furnished credit for the construction of small, one-family houses. At the same time the government sponsored the establishment of "The Mortgage Bank of the Building Industry," co-operatively organized only to the extent that the borrowers became shareholders and had a voice in the management. While the state subscribed to shares of stock in this institution and held the right to appoint three persons to serve on its board of seven, the bank enjoyed an independent status. Funds were

Air view of co-operative housing of A.A.B. at Bronshoj

COPENHAGEN

View of co-operative housing
showing play space in court

Cottage type housing at Bronshoj

COPENHAGEN

Wading pool and sand pile in housing project of the K.A.B. Society

obtained by issuing debenture stock and making short term loans. As a result of the financial aid extended by the authorities, the public utility societies and the "Popular Dwelling" movement showed a rapid development. However, in spite of this building activity over the years, overcrowding is still severe and standards are low both in Helsinki and in the country areas.

Divided broadly, in addition to the ordinary private housing we find three other types in Finland:

CO-OPERATIVE HOUSING SOCIETIES. Dwelling units are rented to members only, but, as previously stated, the development of this form has not been extensive.

JOINT-STOCK HOUSING SOCIETIES. A philanthropic type, somewhat similar to Octavia Hill Association in England and made up of individuals or groups interested in housing reform. In certain cases the municipal authorities are shareholders. The houses built are rented to deserving persons in need of assistance or to the general public.

JOINT-STOCK LODGING SOCIETIES. Organizations or persons who band together and build one or more apartment houses and apportion the space according to the extent of their financial interest. As a rule the shareholders occupy the buildings themselves, but they are at liberty to rent or sell to outsiders any of the apartment units which they may own. The law limits the dividends paid to shareholders in the legally recognized public utility societies. Many of the joint-stock lodging societies exceed this limit and are not classified as public utility housing, but fall into the category of private enterprise operating for unlimited profit. While this type has little social significance, as such, it is the prevailing form of group effort in housing, and consequently a brief description is given.

According to the regulations enforced in most of the joint-stock lodging societies, a member when selling an apartment unit owned by him must first give his fellow members an opportunity to buy it at the market value. If, after a week's time, no member has availed himself of the opportunity, the owner may sell according to his own wishes. In the matter of voting rights, the most common practice is to allow a member as many votes as he holds shares, i.e., one share for each room; some societies base the voting power on the total amount of floor area owned rather than on number of rooms, while others permit only one vote for each member. Members usually hold annual or semi-annual meetings. A board of directors of from four to six members is elected and this board appoints a manager, usually one of the directors, or in some cases from the membership, and he receives a small salary. A caretaker is employed for each apartment house. If the apartment is without central heat, the caretaker receives a wage of from $7.00 to $13.00 a month and his lodgings free and he may engage in outside employment. If the house has central heat, the caretaker's services are fully engaged and he receives a wage of from about $25 to $35 a month and free lodgings.

In the matter of financing during the construction of a joint-stock lodging house, the first mortgage money is borrowed from a private bank or an insurance company on short term notes at 6 per cent to 8 per cent interest. Upon completion of construction this loan is turned into a long term note or mortgage. The second mortgage money is secured either from membership or private sources. There is no tax exemption on buildings or land; the latter is rented from the city on a long term lease. An applicant for membership must make a deposit of a stipulated amount and take out a share or shares. If necessary, it is possible for him to borrow some part of the required deposit by deeding over to a bank his ownership share or shares at market value, varying according to the construction cost of the building. No communal facilities are provided for the tenants by the societies.

The largest of the housing societies embracing a partial social purpose is the Helsinki Workman's Housing Company, Incorporated. Organized in 1920 by the city and operated to earn a limited dividend, it is a half-public and half-private housing society, so designated by reason of the fact that the state and municipality generously subscribed to three quarters of the shares of stock. The Suomi Life Insurance Company and the Housing Reform Society provided funds for the remaining shares. The membership of the Board of Directors is made up of three members appointed by the city and one each from the insurance company and the Housing Reform Society. Shareholders receive 5 per cent dividends.

Between 1920 and 1926 this municipally controlled share company built some 83 frame houses in the Kottby section of Helsinki containing from two to four apartment units each, or a total of 334 dwelling units. Quite simple living facilities were provided for the tenants. Room stoves furnished the heat, and cooking equipment consisted of wood-burning stoves in the kitchens. Rents ranged from $7.00 to $10.50 a month for a one-room and kitchen unit; $11.00 to $15.00 for a two-room and kitchen unit; and around $18.00 for a three-room and kitchen unit. This plain frame housing, now showing the effects of age, does not merit particular praise, but when one realizes that it was erected as an emergency measure to meet a housing crisis it would be unfair to criticize it too harshly.

In 1925, with the purpose of improving upon the emergency measure, the state and the municipality of Helsinki aided in the formation of an organization which built, close to the city, a group of four-story, solid-wall apartment houses. In these buildings apartment units average 430 square feet in area and for the most part are composed of one large room, a kitchen, and a small lavatory containing basin and water closet. Numerous cheap public baths take the place of bathing facilities in the individual apartments. Room stoves provide the heating. Average rents run between $11.00 and $13.00 a month.

Another type of municipally sponsored society for housing the lower income group was founded in 1929. This society built four-story, solid-wall buildings, providing in all some 205 rooms. The financing came from loans from the city, a savings bank, and equity furnished by the occupants. One-room and kitchen apartment units rent for about $15.00 a month. Tenants, by paying an additional $3.75 a month, can acquire the shares held by the municipality, the purpose being to eliminate eventually the city's interest in the housing and turn the ownership over to the tenants. This share company form of half-municipal and half-private housing also exists in the important towns of Turku and Viipuri and in the industrial city of Tampere.

The Lallukka apartment house for artists in Helsinki is not only an outstanding example of philanthropic housing with a distinct social purpose, but also a beautiful expression of modern Finnish architecture. From funds donated by Juho and Maria Lallukka for the purpose of providing studios and low rent dwelling accommodations for active artists and older ones more or less retired, this handsome building designed by Gosta Juslen was erected in 1933. It contains sixteen painters' and four sculptors' studios in combination with one- and two-room with kitchen apartment units. There are also some nineteen two- and three-room with kitchen units and five single rooms. A workshop has been provided for cabinetmakers and a large assembly hall on the first floor gives a place for meetings and entertainments. Occupants of this building include painters, sculptors, actors, and musicians, and the rents are about 25 per cent lower than would be found outside for similar accommodations. For the purpose intended, for the need which was met, and for the beauty of design throughout, this building impressed me as the finest thing of its kind in Scandinavia. From the social angle, there is no justification in providing housing for low income groups and allowing artists to starve in garrets. After all, artists are the torchbearers of culture, which is certainly as necessary to future generations as the products of industrial enterprise.

While the measures taken to relieve the housing shortage in Finland have been beneficial and standards have been thereby improved, due to the increase in population of the cities much remains to be done in housing, particularly for the low income groups. With a well-developed sense of social consciousness and a robust desire to be a progressive state in a modern world, there is every reason to believe that Finland will earnestly strive to make her low rent housing comparable to her social achievements in other fields.

NORWAY

The public authorities in Oslo and other large towns of Norway have been responsible for practically all of the assistance given to the joint-stock housing societies; and in the smaller towns the greater part of this assistance was given to the co-operative societies and to private builders. Credit in the form of guarantees of loans was largely extended through the Norwegian Small Holdings and Dwelling Bank. Exemption from local taxes was adopted by Oslo and one or two other towns to a limited degree.

Among the various forms of housing organizations, the joint-stock housing societies have shown the greatest activity. Many were formed during and after the war and their increase and growth make them the popular type today. As in the other Scandinavian countries, there is a wide difference in their organization and operation. Some are recognized public utility societies with limited dividends. Where these are recipients of municipal aid, thereby being subjected to a limited amount of municipal control, they become the half-public and half-private type of housing society. In fact, since 1929 the participation of the municipality of Oslo in housing has been confined to the formation of this type of stock company in which the city usually has been the principal shareholder. Other housing societies are philanthropic in character, and many are actually private institutions with the profit motive paramount, either selling or renting their dwelling units.

Co-operative housing is of recent origin in Norway and, like the joint-stock companies, assumes many forms. A number of societies collect the savings of their members and apply this fund as necessary equity for the construction of new buildings. Many build only for members, others build for outsiders as well. Some sell the dwelling units in the apartment houses built, while others retain control by renting to members or, as locally expressed, by "giving members the right of permanent occupancy of dwelling units."

The financing of Oslo's half-public and half-private stock company housing is accomplished by securing a first mortgage loan up to 50 per cent of the assessed value of the property from a bank or savings fund society. The second mortgage from 50 per cent to 90 per cent of the building cost, based on what is called "normal value," * is guaranteed by the city. A third mortgage granted by the city completes the financing.

Co-operative and privately organized societies follow the same pattern of financing as it relates to the first and second mortgages, the remaining capital or equity being supplied by the societies or private individuals respectively. For instance, for a one-room and kitchen apartment unit, the equity contributed by a member amounts to from $175 to $275 and for a two-room and kitchen unit the required equity ranges from $375 to $500. In an apartment building in Oslo owned by the

---

* A standard of cost based on an established sum a square meter of gross floor area plus the approved cost of the building site.

Workers Joint-Stock Housing Society, the rent for a three-room, kitchen, and bath apartment unit including heat and domestic hot water ran as high as $27 a month. The tenant had been required to make an equity deposit of $750, a sum much higher than required for similar accommodations in Copenhagen.*

In conclusion, it has been seen that the achievements in public utility housing, so successfully developed in the Scandinavian countries, have taken many and varied forms. This is a normal approach to the solution of the housing problem. "Man is but a reed, the weakest in nature, but he is a thinking reed," says Pascal, and the fact that he thinks and struggles to elevate his economic position brings diversification in his needs and desires. Low cost housing demands a many-sided attack. Various social methods must be utilized with the government providing a standard of attainment not only by publicly constructed projects, but also by its readiness to stimulate and aid group efforts toward self-help. Taken as a whole, public utility housing in its ramifications has played a most important role in meeting the housing needs of a large part of the Scandinavian populations.

* All comparisons in this book are based on the following rate of exchange:

Denmark:	1 krone	= $.23
Sweden:	1 krona	= $.26
Norway:	1 krone	= $.25
Finland:	1 Finnish Mark	= $.02½

4. RURAL HOUSING AND COLONIZATION

THE SCANDINAVIAN COUNTRIES HAVE LONG REC-
ognized that the problem of rural housing cannot be solved
apart from the interrelated factors of improved agricultural
living and income. They considered it impossible to attempt
to rehouse landless tenants and agricultural workers as an isolated measure. Their objective, the setting up of independent
family-size farms, led to the extensive development of the
"small farm holding" movement. This movement may be said
to rest on two fundamental aims: a secure land tenure and a
sound agricultural economy.

In the tenth century in Scandinavia the concentration of
large tracts of land in the hands of the noble families, who re-
fused to divide or sell any part of it, made land shortage
acute. The inability to secure land at home encouraged the
Vikings to engage in foreign conquests bringing about new
settlements and in part solving the land problem of these
pagan warriors. By the middle of the eleventh century the
passion for conquest was mollified by the infiltration of Christianity, and the Viking expeditions subsided. The Danish Viking, Olaf Tryggvasson, after his conversion, promised never
to wage war again on England, and the pledge was kept.

Denmark, Sweden, and Norway at this time were closely
connected and fairly well established as centralized mon-
archies. Their populations were rural, agriculture was the basis of existence, and the peasants possessed a certain amount

of independence. But a scattered rural life made central government difficult. To maintain their position the kings created trained forces of warriors who were required to supply their own military equipment. As compensation for their military services, these warriors, known as "King's Men," were separated from the peasant class and given "fiefs," which for the most part were gifts of land, exemptions from taxes, and local governing offices. Thus a nobility class was born and feudalism established. During the fourteenth and fifteenth centuries feudalism flourished but not to the same extent as in other European countries where serfdom was absolute. Even so the status of the small farmer and peasant changed; they were deprived of most of their former liberty, the small farmer becoming a tenant and the peasant or laborer turning into a serf. Meanwhile the aristocracy steadily advanced; war and commerce brought wealth into individual hands and a powerful class of estate holders arose. Feudal privileges over the peasants grew more rampant. The crown, the nobility, and the clergy were the privileged groups controlling most of the land. The peasants, still the basis of society, paid the taxes, owned little land, and supported the top-heavy structure of feudalism.

The fifteenth century brought a check to the growing power of the nobility in Denmark and Sweden. Attempting to make their class exclusive and increase their political domination they encountered opposition from the crown. For support, the crown turned to the rising burgher or merchant class in the towns and to the peasants in the rural areas. Despite the small advantages brought to the peasants by the crown's favor, their condition for many generations was not nearly so good as that enjoyed by their early ancestors. It was not until the latter part of the nineteenth century that the governments of these countries showed real concern for the evils attending the landless rural populations. Laws were passed directed toward breaking up large estates into small holdings and raising the peasant tenant to the status of small farm owners. By continuing legislation and other assisting measures effected over the years, the small farmer has been enabled to regain his freedom and independence.

Each one of the Scandinavian countries has developed a program suited to its particular needs but the methods used are basically similar. Under the Danish program, tenancy has been reduced to the amazingly small proportion of 6 per cent of the entire agricultural population. In Finland, where tenancy was widespread and acute less than a quarter of a century ago, now 89 per cent of the farms are independently owned. In Sweden 80.4 per cent of the agricultural population own the land they cultivate, while in Norway 85.7 per cent of the farmers are owners. This record is in striking contrast to the situation in the United States where, according to the last census, the proportion of farms operated by tenants has increased from 25.5 per cent in 1880 to 42.1 per cent in 1935.

The successful results in Scandinavia are not due to any natural or peculiarly favorable circumstances, but rather to a wise application of government assistance over a long period of years and still being carried forward. The program is not viewed as an added debt burden on the public but as an effective method of helping people in rural areas to help themselves.

DENMARK'S SMALL FARM HOLDINGS

Denmark is a small country, about equal in size to the combined areas of Massachusetts and New York, and contains a population not much larger than the city of Chicago. Denmark's natural resources are pathetically scarce. Nature tossed her only a few crumbs: a little timber land, some china clay deposits, and a modest assortment of peat beds—in all, not a very generous portion. Iron, coal, oil, and minerals, those resources which nations prize so highly and wage war over, are totally lacking. Agriculture is the chief industry and has so been since earliest times. Eighty per cent of the total area is under cultivation, an unusually large proportion in comparison with other European nations. The climate is not ideal for cultivation; no mountains shut out the cold winds that sweep in from the sea. Despite this fact, Denmark has developed her agriculture intensively and has gained a high world place in the efficiency of her two hundred and five thousand farms. The majority of these farms are classified as *husmand,* or small farm holdings.

The growth of the small farm holding program rose out of the period known as "Denmark's darkest hour," which followed the war with Germany and the resulting loss of Schleswig-Holstein. In addition, between the years of 1860 and 1880 the country lost its grain markets by the competition of the new grain-growing areas of the world. But out of the depths of economic depression and frustration sprang a new national spirit. The Danish leader Grundtvig inspired the people with the expression, "What we have lost abroad we will regain within," and Denmark, discarding dreams of empire status, took steps to put her own house in order. One of the most pressing needs of the hour was relief for the distressed landless population. A wide distribution of independent small farms was considered necessary for rural welfare and tenants were encouraged through various measures to become owners of small holdings. As a result, by 1885 the number of agricultural holdings had reached the total of one hundred and fifty-three thousand. But small farmers needed capital to equip and improve these holdings, and they were compelled to obtain credit from private sources at exhorbitant rates. To relieve this condition the state aided in establishing two small holder credit associations, an act which provided the groundwork for later public measures.

As the start of the actual public program in colonization, legislation was enacted creating a loan fund for capable farm laborers who wished to become independent farmers. But two weaknesses were revealed in this early legislation. First, the amount of the individual loan proved insufficient to buy enough good land for the support of the small farmer and his family, much less to erect a dwelling and the necessary farm buildings. Secondly, the law specified that no additional money could be borrowed until the initial debt was reduced by one half, and this stipulation seriously handicapped the small farmer in securing the necessary working capital. A later law somewhat improved matters by increasing the amount of the individual loan.

But in a system where the guileless prospective small holder was given a cash loan by the state to purchase land, he was easily victimized. The price the prospect had to pay for available land was higher than its market value because the large landowner was aware that he was dealing with an eager buyer using state money and therefore held out for the high price, which he eventually secured. In consequence, the small holder with limited state money at his disposal still found himself unable to secure enough good land to support himself and his family, and as a result he was compelled to go out and work as a laborer, thus defeating the purpose of the law which was to establish independent and self-supporting holdings.

By 1919 criticism of these defects brought about the passage of new and drastic land acts, giving the state power to acquire needed land from the large estates and from the church, and to offer it to small holder applicants on a long-term leasehold plan. The basic policy laid down in these acts was that land should be acquired by the state and made available for subdivision into small holdings; that the leasing of the land should be at a reasonable rate; and that the tenure of the holding should be leasehold so that the holder would be protected from fluctuating land values. Under a rather drastic form of procedure bordering on confiscation, the aggregate amount of estate and church land acquired by this legislation amounted to over 125,000 acres.* For a country the size of Denmark this was a sizable amount of ground.

Prior to the outbreak of the World War, economic conditions were favorable to the middle-sized and the small holder farms, and the latter were steadily increasing in number. But as the war progressed, due to more extensive acreage and grain-growing facilities the larger farms prospered; on the other hand the small holder farms, without the acreage and devoted to breeding and rearing livestock which required imported fodder, suffered. As a result of this unfavorable war condition, the establishment of new small holdings was arrested, and what was even more serious, a substantial number of the small holdings already existing were bought by the owners of large farms and added to their field areas. It was, after all, the old story of land passing into the hands of large estate owners, a practice harking back to feudalism. A homely illustration of this principle may be seen in a simple physical experiment. Pour a few drops of oil on the surface of clear water from a height of several feet. The oil strikes the surface and scatters, forming large and small pools. A curious thing happens: by capillary attraction the large pools irresistibly attract the smaller pools and promptly absorb them. At the end of a few minutes the smaller pools have vanished leaving only a few greatly enlarged pools. So it is with small land holdings without protection. Land gravitates into the hands of the large landowners and the former owners become the laborers and tenants of the new owners—an experience not unfamiliar in the United States, where hundreds of thousands of acres in the West were distributed to settlers under homesteading acts,

---

* By 1939 virtually all of this land had been parcelled out.

only to be absorbed later by large owners—the rapacious jungle overgrowing the unprotected clearing.

To meet the menacing threat of diminishing small holdings, the Danish parliament passed provisional legislation which prohibited the closing down of any existing farm, and in 1925 permanent legislation established the inviolability of the small holdings by the following restrictions: (1) that all existing small farm holdings should be continued as independent units; (2) that each independent holding should have buildings and occupants to cultivate the land; (3) that a holding could not be leased for a period longer than five years except with the consent of the Minister of Agriculture; (4) that a detachment of land from a holding could be made only when the remaining portion of the said holding was large enough to support a family. It was further stipulated that additional land could be added to a holding or that there could be an amalgamation of small holdings, provided in each case that the total area of land joined together would not exceed three hectares or about seven and one-half acres.

The effect of this legislation was to secure definitely the existence of independent small holdings where agriculture was the most advantageous use of the land. It was actually a process of whittling down the large estates, every flying chip taking the form of a new small farm holding.

The fundamentally important legislation enacted in 1919 has been the basis for the later laws of 1934, as modified by the more recent laws of 1936 and 1938. The present small holding legislation, taken as a whole, combines two main features: freehold tenure, as set up in the 1899 act known as "the old law," and state leasehold tenure as established in the 1919 act known as "the new law." An applicant for a small holding is given his choice of the two methods of acquiring land: either, under "the old law" plan, he receives a maximum loan from the State Loan Fund to purchase the particular piece of ground he desires; or, under "the new law" plan, he rents a parcel of state-owned land on a long term lease. The purpose of the government in maintaining the dual plans of land acquisition and tenure is to determine which one secures the greater permanent benefit to the small holder over a period of years. The administration of the small holding legislation is under the Ministry of Agriculture and Fishing assisted by two other agencies of government, the Agricultural Law Committee of the state and the local county commissioners.

An applicant for a small farm is required to be a citizen of the country and between the ages of twenty-one and fifty-five years. He must produce a statement from his local county commissioner and from two reputable persons to the effect that he is sober, honest, and reasonably qualified to operate a small farm. It is necessary that he possess a limited amount of capital but not sufficient to secure a small holding unaided. He cannot own at the time any other piece of ground suitable for a building site or garden lot, and he must have resided in the county for the previous twelve months. The authorities require that the size and condition of the soil be suitable to support a family without outside labor. Under no circumstances can the area of a parcel of land be less than three hectares (seven and one-half acres), and where the soil is mediocre in quality, the size of the parcel may be as large as fifteen hectares (thirty-seven acres). In cases where several applicants desire the same piece of state land, the ablest and thriftiest are favored, but where the choice lies between several good and able applicants, the one with the smallest economic means is selected.

The law provides that small holders under "the new law," or leasehold plan, may secure a loan for buildings up to the cost of construction but not exceeding a maximum sum of 10,000 kroner (about $2,300), provided that three fourths of the members of the Agricultural Law Committee have approved the action. A loan of 8,000 kroner (about $1,840) or under does not require this form of approval. No interest is charged on the loan for the first five years; after this, 4½ per cent interest must be paid semi-annually, of which ½ per cent is applied to amortization of the loan. The postponement of the interest payment is a wise provision in that it frees the small holder from burdensome payments during the difficult initial years on the holding. Where loans are for buildings on land purchased by the applicant under "the old law" or freehold plan, the interest rate is similar to that on state leasehold land. However in this case payments are made during the initial five-year period, and as security for the buildings the state holds a second mortgage on the property. Until only a few years ago the small farm holders were permitted to erect the buildings on their holdings without supervision. This practice resulted in a substantial number of poorly constructed buildings which required expensive upkeep. Therefore the government now stipulates that all small holder buildings must follow plans prepared by architects approved by the government, and that the construction must be supervised.

A rigid stipulation forbids the destruction of the fertility of the soil by the small holder, and the removal of clay, lime, etc., from the surface unless permission has been obtained in advance from the Minister of Agriculture. If the small holding character of a property is changed, all loans become due immediately.

Concerning land, the small farmer who has leased a holding from the state becomes a "proprietor" rather than "owner." He pays to the state as rent in semi-annual payments, 4 per cent of the appraised value as determined by periodic valuations. In contrast, under the freehold plan of acquiring land with a government loan, a prospective small holder may, if he wishes, purchase his ground from private sources. The loan for land cannot exceed its actual cost and is limited to a maxi-

Kanslergaarden housing project on the Borgermester Jensens Alle, a street with lanes for vehicles, horseback riders, cyclists, and pedestrians

New two-story, semidetached, co-operative apartments

Types of housing in COPENHAGEN

Court of the Kanslergaarden project

Co-operative housing for tobacco workers

New apartment buildings of H.S.B., the largest co-operative housing society in Sweden. This type represents the latest development in Swedish apartment house planning

STOCKHOLM

An interior view of an apartment in one of the co-operative houses erected by H.S.B.

mum sum of 8,500 kroner (about $1,955), and as security the
state holds a first mortgage on the property. Interest payments
on the amount of the land loan do not begin until after the
first five years, then 4½ per cent interest must be paid semi-
annually, the ½ per cent representing amortization.

Between the period of 1900 and 1925, some 16,000 small
holdings were established under the freehold tenure system;
during this time the government expended about $23,500,-
000 in loans and grants. And as supplementary loans the government granted over $4,500,000 to some 11,000 small hold-
ers. Up to the year 1935, over 5,269 small farm holdings were
established on state-owned land under the leasehold system
with the state granting loans for buildings to the amount of
$13,000,000. By reason of the fact that the system of freehold
was in operation twenty years before the leasehold plan was
inaugurated, it is not possible to determine any dominating
preference for one system or another. In certain sections of the
country the freehold system is popular while in others leasehold has taken the lead. In the Jutland area the frugal and
more individualistic farmers prefer freehold ownership, while
on the islands where the farmers live a more closely interrelated life, the state's leasehold plan has found greatest favor.

In comparing the two systems of land tenure, many small
holders prefer the freehold plan because they like, among
other things, the prestige attached to the ownership of property, although the benefits are more intangible than concrete.
As opposed to this, other small holders select the leasehold
plan because they prefer not to be exposed to the vicissitudes
of property ownership. They feel that their economic interests
should not be tied to fluctuating land values, but should be
centered on gaining a living from the soil, and that therefore
they are better off as "proprietors" of state land with a stable
long-term tenure. Among the many arguments advanced in
favor of state leasehold for small farmers are the following:

(1) When the state buys and leases the holding, land prices remain more nearly stationary. (2) The small holder obtains through the government's activity and direction an adequate amount of land sufficiently fertile to support himself and his family without being forced to turn to any outside employment. (3) The slender personal means of the small holder is released for the initial operation of his new farm. (4) As his "proprietorship" of the small holding embodies full use of it for his lifetime with the right to leave it to his heirs for the same agricultural use, he is no less advantageously placed in this respect than the small holder who owns his land outright. While he cannot benefit under this plan by any speculative rise in property value, neither is he adversely affected by any decline in value. In other words, his position as an agriculturalist is as nearly stable as is possible, and he rises and falls largely in proportion to his own efforts rather than by the intrusion of those forces relating to land speculation over which he has no control.

Altogether there are now some one hundred and thirty-five thousand small farm holdings in Denmark, each with less than thirty-seven acres of land. Although these holdings occupy only one fourth of the total area of cultivated ground, they accommodate approximately one half the total rural population. The average size is about fifteen acres. Within the past few years the maximum size of new holdings has been increased to about twenty-two acres. Other statistics reveal the significant fact that it is not primarily the sons and daughters of the small holders who migrate to the city, but rather it is the children of farm laborers—an indication of the restlessness of landless agricultural families. Of no less interest is the item from the records of the Danish Bureau of Farm Management and Agricultural Economics showing that small holdings, when not too small, have yielded the largest net profit per acre, as compared with the profits of farms of all sizes. As an extension of the small holding program, the government has been considering the creation of one- and two-acre holdings for factory workers, the land to be cultivated in periods of leisure or unemployment. This purely subsistence form has already been adopted in Sweden.

> "When the sun, turned westward on glittering wheel,
> Casts wide o'er the moorland a shade,
> I straighten my back, and life's purpose I feel,
> As the blue light glows bright on the earth-burnished steel
> Of my shovel, my hoe, and my spade."

So writes Johan Skjoldborg, a poet of the small holders. As a visitor to Denmark, one would miss a very vital part of the housing movement if the small holding program in the rural areas was ignored. To see the small holder farm in operation is to believe in the sterling worth of small independent units.

One fine morning we started out by motor from Copenhagen and drove in the direction of Ringsted. The gently rolling Danish countryside, with its tufts and patches of low-timbered greenery isolated amidst yellow stretches of grain, presented a rather idyllic picture. No mountains or even high hills interrupted the view toward distant horizons. Our road, studded on each side with shapely metal telegraph poles, snaked its way through quaint little villages, by picturesque churches and houses with straw-thatched roofs, and through fields of grazing cattle. Passing carts laden with produce, at length we struck a colony of small holdings near Spanager. Little white farm buildings with their strips of cultivated land flanked both sides of the highway. We stopped in front of a farm house and our guide went in to ask permission to inspect the holding. He returned in a few moments with the information that the men folk were harvesting in the fields—we could see them in the distance—and the wife was hesitant about admitting strangers; she said that if we would come back in the late afternoon when the work was over, there would be a welcome for us. We drove on and stopped in front of another homestead.

This farm house was concealed by fruit trees and tall shrubbery and a high hedge. We were invited in and met the owner and his wife, who had occupied the holding since 1924. After a kind welcome, conducted with some measure of ceremony, we were shown through the house. "Come into the parlor," said our guide, "They want you to see this room." In most cases each little farm house has a "parlor," always kept in the best of order for visitors and seldom used by the owners. This small white solid-wall house, with tiled roof, contained more room area than appeared from the outside. A bedroom had been tucked in a half-story under the roof, and on the ground floor beside "the parlor" was the main bedroom, a living and dining room, a kitchen, a small pantry, and an entrance vestibule. There was modern plumbing and the heating was done by efficient-looking room stoves. Both the house and barn were equipped with electricity. A profusion of potted plants, including some exotic varieties, stood on the window sills.

On our way to the barn we wandered through a crowded garden of both flowers and vegetables. The owner, short and sturdy, dressed in work clothes, wooden farm shoes, and a light grey straw hat, answered with animation all the questions put to him. He told us that his barn with a thatched roof accommodated six cows, two work horses, and a number of pigs, and that he also kept about two hundred chickens. On his eighteen acres he had cultivated the ground in accordance with the lay-out advised for a small farm of this kind, dividing his fields into plots and practicing intensive cultivation with an eight-year crop rotation. The eight fields, on medium soil, had been laid out for: (1) wheat or rye, (2) mangels and other root crops, (3) barley, (4 and 5) clover and pasture grass, (6) oats, (7) root crops, and (8) so-called "mixed cereals." For the most part the "cereals" were a mixture of oats and barley with some vetches. He informed us that he belonged to a number of co-operative societies which gave him a reliable market for his products; his eggs were sold through his local egg co-operative; he sent milk to a co-operative creamery; and his pigs went to the co-operative slaughterhouse where, under a national quota system, he was assured of a standard price for a certain number of pigs marketed during the year. Likewise he bought his farm supplies, seed, and additional feed through another co-operative. His animals looked well cared for, and the place gave the impression that it was in itself a complete working unit. Questioning disclosed that prior to the occupation of his state-aided small holding this man had been a tenant on a large estate, working as a day laborer.

This particular holding proved to be quite typical of others in the colony. In connection with the pigs, I was reminded of a trip we had previously made to one of the large co-operative slaughterhouses where, in the twinkling of an eye, pigs were transformed from their rotund selves into choice Danish bacon. As we approached this slaughterhouse, wagon loads of disconsolate, squealing pigs passed us. It was as though they sensed from a distance the unhappy approach of their demise. It made me think of the tumbrels of the French Revolution filled with victims on their way to the guillotine, save that the poor pigs were denied the acclaim of crowds lining the streets.

In the vicinity of Ryegaard I had an opportunity to see some of the new small holdings, and at one place the buildings were still under construction. The hollow tile exterior wall of the dwelling had just received a white stucco finish. The usual red-tiled roof covered the house, and corrugated asbestos sheet roofing had been laid directly on the rafters and purlins of the barn, the walls of which were constructed of brick with metal windows. The sound construction of these buildings demonstrated the care and attention being given to the building phase of colonization by the authorities.

The plan of the ground floor of the house contained "parlor," bedroom, kitchen, dining room, food storage room, and laundry. The barn, which was quite large, was being fitted out with stalls for eight cows, pens for a number of pigs, stalls for two horses, calf pens, storage spaces for ensilage, hay, and grain, as well as space for wagons and tools. Here the barn was detached and removed by a distance of some fifteen feet from the house, but in many cases it is attached to one end of the house, forming a single unit. No modern plumbing is put in these houses, and the cellars are not excavated. As a rule the attic is not finished, but a sleeping room or two is often placed here at some later date. The house and barn were to be equipped with electricity. It was estimated that the cost of this service for complete farm use would be about $4.25 a month maximum.

In studying the small holder movement and in my conversations with officials here and there, I found emphasis being put on the value of the co-operatives, with often an added assertion that only through co-operation could the small farmers hope to maintain themselves and compete economically with the larger farmers of the community. Co-operation gives the small holder a known market for his products at the best obtainable price and also enables him to buy advantageously. By this collective effort the best agricultural specialists are employed to serve the interests of the small farmers. The joint effort of the different co-operative enterprises results in a high degree of agricultural efficiency, which is not only reflected in the individual but shows its impress on the nation as a whole. Co-operative societies in Denmark have accounted for 49.3 per cent of all butter exported, 75 per cent of all eggs exported, 86 per cent of the bacon output, and 67.4 per cent of the imported feed supplies. Of all farmers in Denmark, 92 per cent are members of co-operative societies, while a third of the entire population purchase consumer goods through co-operative stores.

Sir H. Rider Haggard, the English writer and agriculturalist, as early as 1910 drew attention to the necessity for co-operatives in the life of the small holder. He says, "Were it not for the elaborate system of Danish co-operation he would fail miserably. By co-operation he lives and moves and has his being. . . . The peasant or little farmer who is a member of one or more of these societies, who helps to build up their success and enjoys their benefits, acquires a new outlook. His moral horizon enlarges itself, the jealousies and suspicions which are in most countries so common among those who live by the land fall from him. Feeling that he has a voice in the direction of great affairs, he acquires an added value and a healthy importance in his own eyes. He knows also that in his degree and according to his output he is on an equal footing with the largest producer and proportionately is doing as well. There is no longer any fear that because he is a little man he will be browbeaten or forced to accept a worse price for what he has to sell than does his rich and powerful neighbor. The skilled minds which direct his business work as zealously for him as for that important neighbor." *

Three major factors have made the success of the small holder movement in Denmark. We have mentioned the first as being the state's assistance in acquiring a small holding, and the second as the sustaining force of co-operation. The third factor, which we may introduce as an intangible influence, is the people's college or folk high school, supplementary to the usual agricultural training. These folk high schools have quickened the desire for knowledge among the young men and women in rural areas and made their minds respon-

---

* H. Rider Haggard, *Rural Denmark* (London, Longmans Green and Co., Ltd., 1910).

sive to new ideas. The teaching in these schools has been based on the premise that training in the evaluation of ethical good should underlie technical skill; that education should teach independence and, at the same time, the ability to work with others for the welfare of the community. The folk high school training seems to correct that fault of traditional democracy described by an English scholar as "too individualistic in its educational assumptions." There are now fifty-nine folk high schools in Denmark attended by over thirty-five hundred men and thirty-two hundred women. For many years the state has contributed limited annual grants to the expenses of these schools, both for salaries for teachers and scholarships. In order to secure grants, these schools, private in nature, meet certain general state requirements.

Peter Manniche, the distinguished founder and principal of the International Folk High School at Elsinore in Denmark, accurately describes the effect of the folk high schools upon rural youth: "The people's colleges tend to awaken in these young people an understanding of what the individual owes to the community, a feeling of confidence in others and the will to sacrifice what individual surplus gain might be obtained in private undertakings by joining in common undertakings by which the whole population and, through it, the individual also, is served. . . . The awakening and enlightenment which the whole farm youth of Denmark has received through the people's colleges is the reason why in Danish agriculture there is not so great a distance between the work of the few outstanding agriculturalists and that of the farmers in general. The great mass of the farmers are in a position to follow the pioneers at a quicker pace than was the case before the schools began to work and as is the case in many countries."

In addition to the folk high schools, four schools for small holders have been established through state support to teach subjects primarily of interest to small farmers. The "small holder tours," which give an opportunity to small holders to observe new agricultural methods practiced on other holdings, small and large, have been another potent educational force. To encourage this project the state makes an annual grant toward the expenses of the tours. Still another valuable educational medium has been the local small holder societies, numbering about thirteen hundred in all with a total membership of some eighty-five thousand farmers. Again, the state encourages the efforts of the small holders by making annual grants to further the activities of their societies, which provide advisers, make field experiments, conduct lecture courses, and offer prizes for outstanding cultivation of small holdings.

The small holder plan in Denmark has brought to the small farmer these many benefits: (1) a greater opportunity for the development of the individual; (2) increased security and a higher standard of living; (3) a common workshop where man and wife toil together; (4) an environment where children become an advantage and receive favorable influences for their rearing; (5) the knowledge that the small holder is his own employer and that the more he perseveres the greater will be his harvest; (6) relief from the anxiety of unemployment, since there is always work to do; (7) opportunities for education and stimulating contacts with other small farmers; and (8) co-operative participation.

The state, too, has benefited by the small holding plan: (1) A more stable and responsible rural population has resulted. (2) The extensive participation of small holders in co-operatives has enabled crops to be more readily adjusted to market needs, thus giving better protection to the national economy. (3) By improved farm practices, soil conservation has received its merited attention. (4) Of great importance, heavy relief burdens on the state have been prevented for the future. It is safe to say that none of these benefits could have been secured in the presence of a large landless population.

With the government making available the fertile land and providing sufficient initial tools for production, with the people's colleges and small holder schools providing both inspiration and technical knowledge, and with the co-operatives giving direction and effectiveness to the use of the tools, it can be said, in summary, that a beautiful pattern of rural life unfolds: The small holder lives independently on his holding, he works individually with his tools, and he functions collectively to market his products and to secure the necessities of living. He is not at the mercy of the caprice or greed of any overlord. His rise or fall is in direct ratio to his own ability. In this pattern he fulfils two essential requirements of living: *he goes of himself and he goes well with others.*

SWEDEN'S DIVERSIFIED RURAL PROGRAM

From earliest times agriculture has been the prominent industry in Sweden. As late as the 1870's nearly three fourths of the population gained a livelihood from the soil. In the past fifty years, however, a gradual change has occurred. Industry and commerce have gained an important place in the national economy, causing a large increase in the urban population and a relative decrease of that in the rural areas. Despite the latter fact, agricultural production has actually increased and exceeds domestic requirements.

Peasant farms and small holdings characterize Swedish agriculture. The countryside supports over 430,000 agricultural holdings on a cultivated area of under 9,000,000 acres. Only some 7,700 of these holdings are classified as large estates, each with an area of approximately 125 acres. The great majority of Swedish farms consist of small holdings, numbering over 340,000 and utilizing 34 per cent of the cultivated land. Land division varies in different sections of the country, the larger farms being concentrated in the central and southern parts of Sweden. Four fifths of all holdings are cultivated by owners, the remaining being leased to tenants or "crofters"; on a percentage basis, official reports show that 80.4 per cent are cultivated by owners and 19.6 per cent by tenants.

Like Denmark, Sweden in its earlier history was faced with a deeply entrenched land problem, but since the end of the nineteenth century the authorities have been giving ever increasing attention to the question of land distribution. As larger and larger areas were passing into the hands of sawmills and other industrial enterprises, greater numbers of peasant owners were merging into a class of tenants dependent on industry rather than agriculture. Of the areas already under cultivation, a substantial portion of land was held by large estate owners. Another problem existed in connection with the thousands of laborers employed as foresters who, without access to homeownership, were inadequately housed in temporary shacks. As these problems became acute, the state found itself compelled to take corrective measures.

In developing its program for housing in the rural areas, the state's purpose was not only to keep the rural population in possession of their own land, but also to encourage wider subsistence from cultivation. This meant the creation of new independent holdings and improvement of the older ones. Various means have been taken to meet the diversified needs. Five different programs, overlapping in some respects, have been gradually established and may be characterized as follows: (1) *Subsistence Holdings*, to give forest workers, loggers, farm laborers, stonecutters, and fishermen the opportunity to acquire subsistence holdings from which a part-time livelihood could be secured; (2) the *Own Homes Movement*, to allow persons of limited means to secure loans at low interest rates and with long term payments for acquiring ownership of homes in rural areas, either agricultural small holdings or dwellings; (3) *Housing Renovation and Improvement in Rural Districts,* to provide improvement grants and new construction loans for encouraging building in rural areas; (4) *Farm Workers' Dwelling Loans,* to improve existing dwellings and for the erection of new ones for farm workers, either owners or tenants; and (5) *Leased Own Homes,* to provide small farm holdings to persons of little or no means on leased state land.

Underlying these five programs has been legislation making land available and generally improving the position of landless workers in agricultural areas. As a measure to preserve existing peasant properties, in 1909 a series of laws was enacted limiting the right of companies and other nonagricultural groups to acquire property in both urban and rural areas. By additional legislation, stringent regulations were imposed on landowners, either individuals or companies, who held agricultural land for purposes other than cultivation and residence, the objective being to stimulate the voluntary sale of land to tenants, a purpose largely accomplished. Further, where a holding had been acquired with state assistance but had not been put to the intended agricultural use, an act was passed in 1924 enabling the repurchase of such property by the state.

As early as 1891 the first of these programs came into existence when the Swedish government took the initial steps to provide homesteads for forest workers on state-owned forest land. Leases for these homestead sites were granted for a maximum period of twenty years, lumber for building purposes was donated, tax exemption was allowed, and grants were made to cover initial cultivation costs. In turn, the forest worker was obliged to act as a keeper on the adjoining park lands, and to perform other work for the state. Three years later the state extended the area on which homesteads could be leased to include the wasteland and state parks in the six northern counties. Provision for ownership was made more liberal by increasing the amount of grants for cultivation and cost of buildings. Later regulations were directed toward preventing settlement under conditions unfavorable to cultivation or without access to outside employment, previous experience having demonstrated that placing settlers on part-time holdings without good soil and a reasonable likelihood of employment was disastrous. Under the continued program of settlement, some two thousand forest holdings have been established in the Norrland section of Sweden.

As a continuation of the principles represented by the forest subsistence holdings, the state established a Workmen's Small Holdings Fund in 1933 to be applied to the acquirement of small holdings not only for forest workers but for stonecutters, farm laborers, fishermen, and the like, with a purpose of providing an auxiliary support from subsistence farming. The scope of operations was at first restricted to the district of Norrland and certain other sections, but later was extended to apply to the whole country. Under the latest provisions of this program the state grants loans to applicants out of the Workmen's Small Holdings Fund up to a maximum amount of about $1,550, of which not more than a third can be spent on the purchase of land, the other two thirds being reserved for the construction of buildings. A distinctive feature of these loans is the fact that they may be secured without any contribution from the applicant, since the purpose is to assist persons who may be in a distressed condition without available funds. The total loan is divided into two parts; that used for land is known as the "fixed" part and that for construction of buildings as the "amortization" part. No repayments of loan are required for the first five years, giving the settler an opportunity to become established. Beginning the sixth year, one thirtieth of the amortization part is repaid each year until completed in the thirty-fifth year. After this period, interest is paid on the fixed part of the loan at the current rate established which is usually around 4 per cent.

The local administrative committees base their selection of land on its capacity to support two cows and some domestic animals, the amount needed for this purpose being from five to eight acres of arable ground. Other stipulations regarding choice of land are that (1) it should preferably lie close to other cultivated land, provided the costs for good soil are not too high; (2) it should be accessible to village or community markets and to schools and roads; (3) it should preferably have some land adjoining which could be obtained at some future time if and when the settler might find it necessary to secure his whole support from the holding; and (4) it should possess some woodland, either in the unit itself or not too far removed from it.

The government exercises as much care in securing desirable housing standards for these small subsistence holdings as it does for the larger farm holdings. While construction costs must be minimized, there cannot be any sacrifice of sanitary measures. Some of the requirements include the following: (1) The dwelling house must be separated from the animal barn. (2) The foundation of the house is required to go down below frost level. (3) The first floor must not be less than about a foot above the ground, and total floor area cannot exceed forty-five square meters. (5) All windows should open to give ventilation. (6) The house must contain necessary heating arrangements. The state permits the fixed part of the loan to include initial cultivation costs, roadway building, and the necessary laying of pipe lines, but may not be used for ditches or fences. In a manner similar to the "self-help" houses in Stockholm, the small holder may reduce the amount of his loan by contributing his own labor in the construction work.

This consequently gives him a feeling of greater attachment to the holding.

While the subsistence holdings program was the first to be started in Sweden, the Own Homes Movement initiated in 1904 has assumed the largest proportions of any of the state's rural housing and colonization activities. This movement resembles in a measure the Danish small holder movement in that the aim is to assist persons of very slender means to acquire small holdings in rural areas through the extension of low interest bearing loans and long term repayments. The method of acquiring the land is based on freehold ownership. As an extension of the Danish system, the program divides itself into two parts: loans and grants for the acquisition of small farm holdings where the complete support is derived from agriculture, and nonagricultural holdings where suitable housing is the main consideration. In both cases the law stipulates that the property must be located in a rural area or an area beyond the limits of any planned town.

From the start of the Own Homes Movement in 1904 some eighty thousand holdings have been established through this fund, and of these forty-eight thousand are agricultural. The Own Homes Board, the official body administering the loans, has reported that 75 per cent of all these owners had successfully established themselves and that, where failures occurred, it was largely attributable to adverse personal circumstances. Loans from the Own Homes Board are dispensed by approved local intermediaries, who are usually the provincial agricultural societies assisted by agricultural advisers and representatives of the various parishes. In addition, the local community may act as the intermediary as well as rural housing associations. All of these intermediaries receive the loans upon application and dispense the funds at their own risk and discretion, subject to state supervision.

A wide variety of needs are met under the Own Homes Movement, four types of loans being available: (1) "Land Use Loans" for acquiring farm land; (2) "Dwelling Loans" for the erection of dwellings; (3) "Addition Loans" for acquiring additional land or making improvements to buildings so that a better income can be obtained from a farm; and (4) "Premium Loans" for bringing new land under cultivation and the conservation of existing land through dyking, improvement of pastures, erection of outbuildings or building of manure pits. The "Premium Loans" are actually state grants, being considered repaid when the work is completed; any one loan may not exceed the amount of 1,500 kronor (about $390).

In securing a loan for a new agricultural small holding, the total cost of the desired property cannot exceed a maximum of 15,000 kronor (about $3,900) and, in exceptional cases, 20,000 kronor (about $5,200). For an already established agricultural small holding the maximum loan obtainable is 12,000 kronor (about $3,120) or, in exceptional cases, 16,000 kronor (about $4,160); and for a dwelling property the maximum loan is 10,000 kronor (about $2,600). In the case of an agricultural small holding the maximum loan may run as high as five sixths of its total value; or for a dwelling property as such, up to a maximum of three fourths of the value of land and buildings, either existing or proposed. A loan is made up of two parts; the "redemption part" is two fifths, and the "permanent part" is three fifths of the loan. For an agricultural small holding the prevailing interest on the "redemption part" is 3.6 per cent, while the interest on the "permanent part" is 4 per cent. For a dwelling property loan the interest is 4 per cent on the "redemption part" and 4.5 per cent on the "permanent part."

It will be seen that the interest rates favor the small holding which is to be used for agricultural purposes, since the cash income of the owner who farms is likely to be less than that of an owner engaged in some outside commercial or industrial occupation. Due to fluctuating economic conditions, the state at times has found it necessary to exercise a certain degree of leniency. Following the depressed period of agriculture after 1930, borrowers found it difficult to meet interest and amortization charges and the state allowed maturing "redemption" payments to be extended and paid along with the interest on the "permanent part" of the loan. This emergency measure is still in effect.

In an application for a loan by a prospective holder, the state requires that the intermediary investigate suitability of soil, price of land, and proposed buildings. The personal qualifications of the applicant are also carefully examined. He must be a Swedish citizen at least twenty-one years of age and known for his "frugality, sobriety and honest dealing." He must be in need of an Own Homes loan and possess some small amount of capital to supplement the assistance given by the state. In the case of an agricultural small holding he should be experienced in farm work and have the assistance of a capable wife. Since the character and known ability of the applicant carries more weight than the capital he possesses, the state's requirements are flexible and are considered as suggestions to the local intermediaries.

As a measure to combat unemployment and at the same time to increase the number of habitable dwellings, the state in 1933 made a fund available for improvement grants and new construction loans in the rural areas and in densely populated communities, the third of Sweden's five programs. The regulations for improvement grants stipulate in general that the grants must be kept under 50 per cent of the cost of the improvement and not exceed 1,000 kronor (about $260) for a dwelling unit. The new construction loans are subject to 4 per cent interest, expire in twenty years and must not exceed 70 per cent of the building cost or 80 per cent including the improvement grant. The maximum amount of the construction loan is 3,000 kronor (about $780), and where an improvement grant is included, the maximum amount is 2,000 kronor (about $520) for each dwelling.

This program is directed by the state Own Homes Board and functions with the local health committees and committees of the agricultural societies. Administration costs are met by state funds, except that each local community defrays the costs of its own health committee. Under this Own Homes Board program some thirty-two thousand dwellings have been improved.

In 1935 the government established a loan fund to encourage the erection of new farm dwellings or to improve existing dwellings for farm workers. These farm workers' dwelling loans are available to either owners or tenants. The maximum loan for a dwelling is 3,000 kronor (about $780) and cannot exceed 70 per cent of the estimated cost of the whole construction work. This loan is subject to 3.6 per cent interest to be amortized within twenty years. As security for one of these loans, a mortgage up to five sixths of the property must be provided.

The state-leased small holdings program corresponds very closely to the Danish small farm holding program under the leasehold system. It is one of the latest colonization plans initiated by the Swedish government, having been set up in 1934 as an outgrowth of the colonization work originally undertaken by the husbandry or agricultural societies. These husbandry societies, long established in the communities, undertook in 1905 to act as agents for the state in dispensing funds for the creation of small farm holdings. At this period the state exercised very little control over the colonization activities, its part being merely to lend the money, while the selection of the applicants for the small holdings was left to the local husbandry committees.

The next step in the developing program was that these committees were provided with money by the state to buy land for holdings. But faults and abuses gradually crept into the system. Poor soil was purchased, often in inaccessible sections not conveniently located for markets. And often too high a price was paid for the land by the committees, with personal considerations influencing their decisions. Further, undesirable and inexperienced families were placed on the holdings in order to relieve the local community of the burden of support. This unsatisfactory situation was one of the reasons leading up to the adoption of the state-leased small holdings program. Another consideration was a desire to make use of the good soil on abandoned estates. A still more important purpose was to check the unemployment caused by the migration from country to the city, and to put into practice the basic idea that farmers as independent tillers of the soil form the backbone of the country.

Under the new program established more or less experimentally in 1924, the state acquires needed land for small farm holdings through the State Land Authority which is under the Agricultural Department. Land is made available from two sources: either the state purchases farms and estates in the open market, or furnishes suitable state land. The state then subdivides the acquired land into small farm parcels and equips each parcel with the necessary buildings before it is leased and occupied by the small holder. The state extends an equipment loan to the small holder for purchasing implements, seed, fertilizer, and fodder. The small holder under the state leasehold plan enjoys the full rights of proprietorship including that of inheritance—that is to say, the farm can be kept in the family and handed down from father to son.

The initial lease period is five years, and in this period the rent is paid in the form of a low interest on the total sum invested by the state in the holding. After the five year period the state's investment is amortized within ten years; where the small holder has not been able to establish himself and meet his amortization payment, he may secure a renewal of the five-year lease terms—in other words, pay interest charges only. Later if he has met all of his amortization payments he can secure outright ownership of the holding. In this last provision, permitting ultimate freehold ownership, the program departs from the continued leasehold system in force in the Danish plan.

In Sweden I had opportunity to see one of the newest leasehold colonies. On one of those wet chilling days when the blood stream congeals and rheumatism strikes between the shoulder blades, we took an early morning train from Stockholm to Uppsala. The colony of small holdings was located some four miles in the country. On the way it began to snow, and when we arrived in the quaint old university town an icy slush lay over the sidewalks and streets. Our Swedish interpreter was profuse in his apologies for the atrocious weather and kept assuring us that the state of affairs was most accidental and unusual. Having failed to bring an overcoat, his indigo lips and shivering frame lent no uncertain sincerity to his remarks. The local agricultural supervisor met us at the station, fortunately with a closed car, and we battled our way through a sleet storm and over muddy roads to the colony at Jälla Säteri.

The land for this small holding colony had been purchased by the state the year before and developed into twelve self-contained small holdings which were leased to the occupants under the state-leased small holdings plan. The land was part of the original estate belonging in its earlier history to Queen

Christina of Sweden. Down through the years parcels of the large estate had been whittled off leaving finally some five hundred acres of arable land and an equal amount of forest land available for this development. The holdings had been equipped the previous year with frame cottages and substantial-looking barns. Each farm unit followed about the same design but the sizes of the holdings differed slightly in size. We stopped in front of the cottage of Artur Eriksson, small holder, and mushed our way through mud and pools of water to the house.

The family, consisting of Eriksson, his wife, and small boy, were gathered in the kitchen warming themselves around a combined wood- and coal-burning stove. We were shown over the cottage. In one corner of a dry cemented cellar was a large pile of potatoes and other vegetables, part of the winter's food supply. The first floor, which measured 24 feet by 30 feet, contained a kitchen, one large sleeping room, a smaller room, and a concealed stairway going to the attic above. The attic was unfinished but large enough to accommodate a couple of sleeping rooms. The government's purpose here was to let the small holder through his own work provide accommodations for his children or, as expressed to me, for needy relatives. The kitchen stove was equipped with a water back for heating hot water for domestic use, an added convenience which seemed most appropriate for this type of cottage. Two radiators, one in each room, had been hooked up to the kitchen boiler. There were no toilet facilities in the house. A hand pump connected to a well outside, with a pipe line to the barn, furnished water. Electricity for both house and barn was supplied from a state-owned power company at a cost to the small holder of approximately $16 a year. The barn with a floor area measuring 32 feet by 100 feet was divided into two sections, one for the livestock and the other for hay storage and wagons. This building was substantially built with concrete floor and gutters and solid walls for the part containing livestock.

We returned to the warm kitchen for a talk with the family. Eriksson in a low voice, evidently subdued by our presence as strangers, gave us an account of his settling on the holding. He had formerly been a laborer on a big farm not far distant and had only moved to the place some six months before. He had about eighteen acres of pasture and arable land on which he raised during the past growing season potatoes, rye, spring wheat, and oats. His livestock consisted of five cows, one calf, four pigs, two horses, and about twenty-five chickens. He sold the milk and produce through private markets in Uppsala. There was a farmers' co-operative organization in the vicinity but he had not as yet joined. As rent for the land he paid annually to the government 2¼ per cent to 3 per cent interest on its appraised value as farm land and, as rent for the buildings, 3 per cent a year on the cost of their construction. Local real estate taxes were paid by the state, but he and his wife each were required to pay a personal income tax.* I asked Eriksson how he liked being an independent small farmer and if he felt he was going to prosper. His reply was that he had made a living so far, liked it, and hoped that he "could make a go of it."

Leaving this little farmstead which we had seen under very unfavorable weather conditions we looked at other holdings in the settlement. Two rather interesting aspects came to light. Women who had been employed as milkers for the past thirty years on the old estate were lodged in attic apartments in some of the cottages and helped with farm work on the holdings, thus preventing their being forced on local relief. The other aspect related to the amazing increase in the

---

* In view of the extensive services of a social nature provided to their peoples by the Scandinavian governments, the annual per capita tax is remarkably small: Sweden, $26.67; Denmark, $29.06; Finland, $5.80; and Norway, $25.82, as compared to $24.21 in the United States.

productivity of the land. The old estate had carried only 17
milking cows, but under the division into small holdings, 120
cows were now being maintained, and the production of grain
on the same area had increased by 50 per cent. By breaking
this old estate up into small holdings and giving direction to
its cultivation, the means had been provided to support a far
greater number of people than under the previous single
ownership. And twelve families had been established as independent "proprietors" of the land they tilled.

Later in Stockholm I talked to Director Nils Collin, the en-
ergetic administrator of the state's leasehold program, mentioning that the local agricultural supervisor in Uppsala had
stated that eight out of twelve small holder families in the
Jälla Säteri colony were making good and asked him what
the state proposed to do with the other four families. He replied, "That is a problem, but due to the fact that these four
families were laborers on large farms only a year ago I feel
they have not had time to become adjusted to their new
status as operators of their own farms. I think we cannot
fairly judge their performance as yet. We must give them a
longer trial period." He spoke enthusiastically about this state
leasehold plan and said that it had assumed an important
place in the program of rural housing and colonization. The
present trend of the government seems to be toward co-ordi-
nation of the different rural housing activities into a more
unified program.

As in Denmark, co-operation and adult education have
been beneficial influences in maintaining the independence
of small farmers in Sweden. Although the co-operative movement was first initiated by the industrial population, its progress in recent years has been gaining an ever increasing support from the rural population. Numerically, two thirds of the
co-operative societies are in rural areas of Sweden. Ten per
cent of the total retail trade of the country is conducted

through the consumer co-operative societies which, by means of strong organization, have been of inestimable value to the small farmer by reducing the price of such necessary commodities as shoes, rubber goods, coffee, flour, and foodstuffs. Similarly, strong organizations of producer co-operatives have been formed to market the products of farmers, both large and small, being responsible for nearly 90 per cent of the country's entire milk production, 25 per cent of all meat and pork slaughtered, and 50 per cent of the total egg export. Some eight hundred co-operative societies supply credit for agricultural purposes, and approximately eighteen hundred co-operative associations, formed during the past twenty years, distribute electricity. These co-operatives have all helped to fortify the small holder against many of the economic vicissitudes of farming.

An important influence on the small farm holder in Sweden has been the growth of people's colleges, a prototype of the Danish folk high school from which the inspiration was received. In Sweden, however, the development has been along civic and cultural lines rather than along the religious and national lines of the Danish folk schools. The purpose in the people's colleges has been to instill in the rural population a greater civic consciousness and understanding of public affairs, leaving vocational training to other types of institutions. Beginning in 1868, the number of people's colleges has now grown to fifty-six, serving both rural and urban populations. In recent years the sons and daughters of small holders and farm laborers are attending these colleges in increasing numbers. The usual age for students is between eighteen and twenty-one years. In concurrence with the state's policy of encouraging adult education, the people's colleges receive a certain measure of state support and are under the general supervision of the Education Board. The Swedish government has found that adult education, in addition to co-operative activity, increases the likelihood of the small holders' success.

COLONIZATION IN FINLAND

Rural housing in Finland is identified with a broad state program of improving the position of the farmer, particularly the small holder. Recent chapters in the history of the country tell a story of the farm tenant's liberation and his rise to the ownership of an independent agricultural holding.

Early in 1600 when Finland was under Sweden, nobles of the latter country were given extensive grants of Finnish land. The peasants who occupied this land were burdened with a payment of land taxes and became, in fact, tenants of the nobility. By 1654 as much as three fifths of the land in Finland had passed into the hands of these nobles. Increasing taxation further weakened the whole farming class, causing many to lose their land to the owners of the large estates. This feudalistic condition brought intense suffering. Agriculture was primitive, the population poor, and crop failures led to famine and epidemics which killed off more than a quarter of the population. "Be a cow and you will be taken care of, but a man or a horse has nothing to hope for" was the old Finnish saying. Around the middle of the sixteenth century, with the growth in mercantilism and the increase in population, land reforms were undertaken by the creation of new farms and dividing village land into strips for individual ownership. But the manorial estates, exempt from taxation, soon swallowed up most of this newly distributed land and became still larger.

In 1809 Sweden surrendered Finland to Russia, and with the continued servitude of the peasants, by 1865 a still larger number of landless persons were living in poverty and suffering. During this time, the problem of land remained a burning question. Throughout the nineteenth century the subletting of portions of large farms had become quite common. Two main types developed: one, farms, or crofts, with a considerable amount of land, and the other dwelling or "cottage" holdings with little or no land. Both croft and cottage holdings were entitled, under their leases, to obtain timber from the forests of the main farm and to use its pasture land. However, when the forests became valuable and machinery came into use around the beginning of the twentieth century, the estate owners grew unwilling to renew leases with the crofters and cottagers, compelling them to vacate. As a result, the croft system declined to an alarming extent and the former tenants became laborers. At that time only 24 per cent of the agricultural population owned their land. No relief occurred in the declining ownership of farms until the separation of Finland from Russia and the establishment of the independence of the republic in 1918.

One of the first major acts of the new Finnish government was to start a program of transferring ownership of farms to the landless tenants and laborers. By 1934, some one hundred and eighty-eight thousand leased holdings had been transferred to former tenants, sixty-five thousand of them being agricultural; and thirty-one thousand new farms were created as well as land added to twelve thousand and five hundred farms. In all, a transference of some two million acres of land had taken place. Today 89 per cent of all farms in Finland are independently owned, more than five times the number existing independently in 1900.

Despite the rapid infiltration of industry during the past quarter of a century, the agricultural population still constitutes almost two thirds of the total number of inhabitants in Finland. The few existing large farms of over two hundred and fifty acres comprise only 6.1 per cent of the total field area. Land ownership is now divided among a great number of small and medium-sized farms. Of the six hundred thou-

sand land holdings in the entire country, some 61 per cent,
or considerably more than half of the cultivated area, consists of small and medium-sized agricultural holdings of from
seven to sixty acres each. Numerically the largest single group
is that of the independent small farm holding with from ten
to twenty-five acres; these comprise 27 per cent of the whole.
Many of the smaller holdings have so little arable land that
it is necessary for the holder to engage in some outside employment, which, especially in northern Finland, takes the
form of forest work; the holding in this case has a subsistence
value and substantially supplements the income. Even in the
larger holdings, timber land is almost as essential a part of
the farm as field and cattle since large quantities of wood are
used for buildings, fuel, and fences.

The land reform law of 1918 dealt with the redemption of
leasehold properties, transferring them to freehold. Having
taken this initial step the government decided to expand the
program, expressing this point of view: "It has been found
necessary to continue the work of colonization because a
numerous landless population, under restricted economic
conditions, is receptive to revolutionary propaganda." As a
practical answer, the government passed the comprehensive
colonization law, called *Lex Kallio,** in 1922. This law formu-
lated the general principles of colonization and the creation
of farms and small holdings, and constitutes the structure on
which the land settlement program for rural areas has been
built.

This law with its more recent modifications directs that
both state and local assistance be extended to worthy applicants who are in need of: (1) a small farm holding consist-

---

* Kyosti Kallio who prepared the legislation and gave it its name was
then Minister of Agriculture for Finland. Of peasant stock, he began his
public career early and served as Minister of Agriculture under several governments and also served as president. A consistent champion of the welfare
of the Finnish rural population, he was again elected President in 1937.

ing of an area large enough under proper cultivation to support wholly a medium-sized family, and with enough forest land to satisfy normal requirements; (2) additional land to be added to an existing holding to make it an independent farm as described under (1); or finally (3) a small subsistence holding consisting of a homestead with enough land for a vegetable or kitchen plot, the maximum size being about five acres.

This program is administered by a State Board of Colonization and fifteen supervisors, each covering a specified district. Functioning with the state board are over five hundred local boards of colonization, elected by local community councils to which both owners and landless persons belong. The local boards receive and make recommendations to the state board regarding the qualifications of the applicants, the availability of land, and other matters connected with the program.

In order to make land available for purposes of colonization, one of the important features of the law includes the right of expropriation of land by the state under certain restrictions. It seemed that in the past lumber companies had been acquiring arable land as well as forest land from small farms, and they had been permitting the arable land to fall into disuse; certain organizations and groups had been acquiring arable land for speculative purposes; further, many estate owners had in their possession large areas of arable land not being farmed. The general purpose therefore was to bring about a more effective use of the land and to put it into the hands of a larger number of people. The aim of the law, to make land available, was accomplished not so much through use of the power of expropriation, which actually proved cumbersome in execution, but through the threat of its use. In many vicinities large owners were induced voluntarily to sell their land either directly to the aspiring small holder or to the government. Adequate land thus became available.

In acquiring land with state funds, the Colonization Board buys in the open market at reasonable prices and pays in cash. State funds may be used to acquire the land and construct both the dwellings and barns for livestock but cannot be applied toward the erection of an isolated outbuilding. The maximum amount of loan available to the applicant is not fixed by law, since the purpose is to establish a qualified family on the land according to their reasonable needs as determined by both the state and local colonization boards. The average loan is about $600 and in exceptional cases may be as high as $2,500. The small holder pays to the state in interest and amortization charges 4 per cent of the amount of the loan, with the important exception that the first ten years is considered a trial period in which all payments are waived. At the end of the ten-year period, if he has performed his work diligently and been reasonably successful he becomes a so-called "proprietor," and starts his payments to the state which, if paid fully for another thirty-one years, makes him outright owner of the property.

According to the conditions subscribed to by the applicant, the state has precedence in repurchasing the property if and when the owner later wishes to sell, paying to the owner the original cost plus the appraised value of any improvements. In the event the state does not desire to buy it, the small holder may sell to an outsider. If a small farmer who has acquired his property sells it to an outsider for speculative purposes, thereby disregarding the agricultural purpose of the holding, he is subject to a fine of 25 per cent of the appraised value of the holding as such, and in addition, 40 per cent of the appraised value of the ground. Furthermore, he forfeits the privilege of ever again acquiring property through state aid. Confronted with this severe penalty, cases of speculation in state-aided holdings are extremely rare.

The size of holdings varies according to the requirements of the small holder and his family as well as the section of the country. In the northern part of Finland where forest work is the chief occupation and furnishes the major part of the income, the subsistence holdings are about five acres in size. There are many small farm holdings in south Finland without woodland, and the size of these range from about twenty-five to forty acres. The typical size of a farm holding which is more or less self-sustaining may run from twelve to twenty-five acres of arable ground, and where woodland is included the total size may be from fifty to one hundred acres. Under the Colonization Act the maximum allowable size is one hundred acres.

An applicant for a small holding under the colonization law must be a citizen of Finland and at least twenty-one years of age. He must not have committed a criminal offense involving a second loss of his civil rights (so phrased as to not exclude those who may have lost citizenship status by participation in the civil war of 1918), and he cannot be in a position of owning land or otherwise able to acquire a property by his own means. If no dwelling exists on the holding he is required to erect one within three years after securing the property. Also, if the property is a farm holding he must undertake its cultivation. In obtaining a small holding, the applicant is not compelled to advance any money for land and buildings, but he is required to possess reasonable knowledge of agricultural operations and have sufficient means or credit to supply himself with necessary stock and equipment. In northern Finland the amount needed for this purpose runs from $115 to $225, and in the south where the holdings are full-time agricultural holdings, the sum varies between $225 and $700. In allocating a small holding or dwelling site preference is given to those applicants who live in the particular locality. After acquiring a property, the small holder can increase its size within limits at his own expense. Regardless of the fact that he is the recipient of government assistance he is required to pay both local and state taxes, which in view of his circumstances are small. When a loan is applied for, the type of buildings proposed must be approved by the local colonization board. Suggested plans of small holding buildings are available at the central office for a small service cost. Over 117,000 small holders have received financial assistance from the government and of this number 43,322 have paid off their debt to the state and are now full owners of their property.

Averaging the country as a whole, the source of income on a holding of from twenty-five to forty acres is divided as follows:

Source	Per Cent
Cows (butter and cheese)	51
Pigs	11.4
Other animals, as sheep	3.1
Field products	13.5
Eggs (and some poultry)	17.9
Miscellaneous products	3.1

Co-operation in many fields has been the lifeblood of the small farm holder in Finland. By membership in co-operative societies the rural population, and particularly the small holders, has been able to enjoy advantageous buying and selling, enabling them to obtain a reasonable livelihood. By working together through the co-operative societies the small farmers have had access to large agricultural machinery for common use, and have been able to obtain the best pedigreed stock for the breeding of cattle. Through co-operation, electric and telephone services have been brought to the small farms, flour mills and sawmills have been operated, bridges built, water lines laid, and many other services provided in isolated sections. Also, in addition to the government's aid in colonization, co-operative credit societies have made loans to thousands of farmers for the enlargement of their holdings and the creation of new homesteads.

The growth and accumulation of deposits of these credit societies seem to promise that this sphere of co-operation will develop a colonization program in the future. In other words, farmers themselves by the use of their own co-operative banking facilities will to an increasing degree help their own group to become independent farmers. The extent of the use of co-operation in Finland is best shown by a few of the actual figures: these societies account for 38 per cent of all eggs exported; 35 per cent of the cattle slaughtered; 40 per cent to 50 per cent of the grain marketed; 58 per cent of the cheese (commonly found in many stores in the United States under the name "Valio"); 45 per cent of the agricultural machinery purchased; and 40 per cent of the total fertilizers and cattle food sold in Finland. Co-operative retail stores are widely scattered throughout the parishes.

Early one Sunday morning under the cloudless sky of a fresh autumn day we left Helsinki by motor for a trip into the rural areas of Finland. Accompanying us were Dr. O. W. Willandt, Director of the Research Bureau in the Pellervo Society,° and a Mr. Raimo, adviser to small holders. Driving northward, the concrete highway soon dissipated itself into a rather dusty clay and gravel road. We sped through forests

---

° The purpose of the Pellervo Society has been to improve the economic conditions of the Finnish farmers. Its founder, the late Professor Gebhard, is called "the father of the co-operative movement in Finland" and at one time was President of the Central League of Small Holders. The educational activities of the Pellervo Society among the rural people are considered in no small measure responsible for the rapid growth of rural co-operation in Finland.

STOCKHOLM

Single houses at Kvarnholmen, for employees of K.F., a consumers' co-operative society

HELSINKI

New apartment house design found in the outskirts of Finland's capital

STOCKHOLM

Apartment building erected by the employees of the Vartan Gas Works. The whitish-gray finish on the walls is relieved by bands of buff color around the entrances to apartment units

HELSINKI

A studio apartment in Lallukka, a philanthropic housing project built for artists and musicians

of pine and spruce, which gave a pleasant resemblance to the beauty of the Adirondack woods. Granite outcroppings at every turn indicated the difficulties of highway construction. The road grew more hilly, winding its way through small clearings, skirting the sides of small lakes. In these clearings one glimpsed solitary little farm holdings with frame buildings, some simple, unpainted, and primitive, others larger and of no particular style but rather picturesque with their red-painted sides and white trimming. On restricted pasture areas, snatched from the encroaching forest, were cattle of a Guernsey strain. In some places families, including children, were digging potatoes on little patches of land. Dr. Willandt apologized for the Sunday work by saying, "The day is so fine they feel it is a good time to get their potatoes in." A gridiron of ditches spaced some twenty feet apart indented the cultivated fields, this laborious work being necessary to take care of the drainage from the winter snows; otherwise the ground would be too soggy for spring ploughing.

Occasionally we passed youngsters on bicycles and older folk sauntering along in their neat Sunday clothes. Only a few automobiles and one or two busses were on this main highway. On several occasions trucks filled with young boys and girls passed us and we were informed that they were steering their course by compass to an unknown destination—a popular week-end pastime with the young people. The forests began to open up into larger stretches of cleared and cultivated land. We drove through small villages consisting of a few unpainted wooden houses, sometimes with a co-operative store in the center. In Lohja we stopped at the ancient church dating back to the fifteenth century. Between two square granite piers a wide pathway led to the picturesque front entrance. The entire interior of the church, walls and ceilings, were decorated with primitive Biblical figures in color—an impressive sight. The morning service was in progress. We stood inside the doorway in quietness for a few minutes and listened to the village folk chant their prayers. Black bands of cloth strung at the entrance of pews indicated a recent funeral. Returning to the car we traveled farther northward and at length stopped at one of the small holdings.

Kilko Nurmi, owner of the holding, was a gaunt, determined-looking man, yet his face showed kindliness. His wife seemed older. The daughter, Sunday-dressed, had an alert, vivacious manner. We were led into the house, stepping across small spruce boughs flattened fanwise at the entrance as a doormat—a quaint and practical device common to these small farms. Nurmi had been a tenant farmer six years before. The appraised value of his place amounted to about $1,633, of which some $730 represented the value of the land. He had acquired the place through government aid, and in the six-year period of his ownership he had paid off all indebtedness except an amount of $350. He expected in a few years to complete his payments. His twenty-two acres of land were divided into a vegetable garden of half an acre, nine acres of cultivated fields, one and a half acres of pasture, and the remaining eleven acres in woodland. This man was a very thrifty farmer, bringing everything possible into production for income. Chickens, eggs, a pig or two, milk, and some fruit were all produced in excess of the family needs and marketed. In the previous year from his holding he had secured a net income of $373 over and above the living of the family.

He had a small but well-built barn of solid-wall construction for the first floor, a good chicken house, one or two small outbuildings, and last but not least a typical little Finnish bathhouse which really deserves a passing note of description. This bathhouse, common to Finnish farms regardless of size, was a one-room building with an open brick stove at one end for heating the stones upon which water was thrown to provide the steam for the bath. The wooden walls, blackened by smoke, enclosed at one end a platform with a long bench for the "sweating out" process. A towel or two hung over the rail and a couple of birch leaf bundles were lying on the platform steps. Above all, a fragrant odor of birch leaves and stale wood smoke permeated the air. The bath had taken place the evening before. So important is this steam bath that the Finns have an old saying, "When the bath and brandy fail, death is at the door!"

The main house was quite old. The spacious combined kitchen and living room, with a log-beamed ceiling, contained a brick stove in one corner for cooking and heating the room in the wintertime. Wide floor boards, partially covered with long strips of homemade rug, creaked a bit as we walked over them. Typical farm-house pictures were hung on the wall, simple oil scenes, chromos and enlarged photographs; and several framed certificates indicated proficiency in agricultural ability. One large certificate, embellished with a picture of a man and boy ploughing, designated proficiency in beet-growing. While superficially the cash earnings of this small holder did not seem large, his net income of $373, in addition to the family's attractive work surroundings, security, and good life, seemed infinitely preferable to the existence of a tenant farmer living in the midst of insecurity, malnutrition, and bad housing.

We drove on to another small holding some miles distant. This second place had a very attractive setting between two hills with a distant view over a long, cleared, undulating stretch walled in by evergreen forests. A road trailed off down the clearing, in gentle rises and falls. The family was composed of the small holder, his wife, and two children. He was a young man between twenty-five and thirty, tall, lean, clear-eyed, with quite a handsome face, his attire noticeable by the new black leather boots he wore. She was smallish, homely, with high cheek bones and hair brushed back close to her head exposing the forehead. We were invited in to the "parlor" and were served a reddish local berry drink with sugared cakes, very refreshing and tasty. Besides the "parlor," kitchen, and a bedroom on the first floor, the house contained three bedrooms on the second floor, all with rather meager furnishings in them. A large T-shaped barn provided space for the livestock. This small holder owned four cows, four pigs, a calf, and some one hundred and seventy chickens, but had no horses, his land being ploughed by arrangement with a neighbor. There were ten acres of arable ground and fifteen acres of timber in his holding. He marketed his milk, the chief source of his income, through a co-operative dairy, but explained that he sold his eggs locally because the egg co-operative was too far away. He had no regular income from his timber. On the appraised value of his holding, amounting to about $1,650, he paid 5 per cent interest on the $350 which he had borrowed from the state under the colonization program; the remainder of the capital in the place was made up of his personal funds and money obtained from a co-operative credit society. In annual taxes, he paid $5.85 to his local community, $7.00 to the state, and about $2.32 as voluntary contribution to his church, a total of $15.00.

A short distance away at a larger farm holding the owner's income was derived from diversified sources, agriculture supplemented by sale of timber, some outside employment, and the serving of meals. This family made their own soap, did some weaving of Finnish cotton for their own use, and produced a portion of their other household needs. We had a sumptuous lunch at this farm, sitting down to a long table spread with all manner of country dishes including smoked fish, salted meat, boiled potatoes, hot macaroni, cole slaw, beet and potato salad, two or three kinds of Finnish bread, large pitchers of milk, plates of butter, and an apple junket dessert. After a needed rest and conversation with the owner we went on for some distance under a bright sun beginning to turn down toward the forest horizon.

Leaving the main road, we turned left over a frail-looking bridge and in a few minutes came to a small farm holding perched on rising ground giving uninterrupted view of a lake in the distance. It was a pretty setting: the Finnish flag fluttering from a pole, the house in the midst of a garden of flowers and fruit trees, and the whole enclosed by a white rail fence. The only object marring the scene was the customary disfiguring ladder leaning against the eaves to give quick access to the roof in case of fire. The owner and his wife met us at the entrance gate. His Voltarian face readily seamed itself in wrinkles when he smiled. He took us first to his cattle barn, a long low building concreted inside and containing the usual stalls and pens for livestock. At the end of the building, a large storage space was half filled with dried moss used as bedding for the animals. There was a fairly large chicken house and a completely filled hay barn containing a room at one end where grain was being dried. He showed us his meadowland, about three acres in extent, where tiling was being laid for underground drainage. This was an improvement on the open ditching method of field drainage and when completed, he said, would increase his yield from the meadow at least 10 per cent. To encourage farmers in making this improvement, the state gave a grant of money for the installation of drainage tiling. This small holder was receiving about $140 from the state toward a total estimated cost of $175 for the work.

With true rural hospitality we were invited into the parlor of the farm house for refreshments. A scarcity of ready chairs created a momentary flurry until more were brought down from the second floor. Without screens in the windows a goodly number of houseflies, international in character, were buzzing around and settling on a heaped-up dish of cakes in

the center of the table, but no one seemed to show any concern about this unsanitary touch. The wife and daughter
brought in the coffee which lacked a measure of virility. The
muffled sound of a radio floated down from the floor above.
The married daughter, a pretty blonde type with a strong
lithe figure, swept silently in and out of the kitchen replenish-
ing the refreshments. It seemed that she and her husband
lived and farmed with the parents, but the husband was away
on his required military service.

This small farm gave every indication of being efficiently
run. The owner had formerly been a tenant farmer, but by his
enterprise had paid off all his indebtedness and now owned
his place. His livestock consisted of seven cows, two horses,
seven pigs, and from sixty to seventy chickens. He and a
neighboring farmer owned their water supply jointly. The
holding was supplied with electricity generated by a co-operative power plant, which had a membership of two thousand
farmers; this same co-operative also operated a local sawmill
and grain mill. For bringing the electrical line to his farm the
small holder had paid about $70, and his cost for current ran
about $14 a year. His telephone service was supplied by an-
other co-operative at a low rate.

We now turned homeward. Lengthening shadows cast by
the evergreens fell across the road. The air grew crisper. We
passed a few lakes, some close at hand, others in the distance.
After an hour and a half's drive we reached the outskirts of
Helsinki. People walking, on bicycles, on motorcycles, were
returning to the city after a gorgeous October day in the country. We had seen sturdy independence and good living among
small farmers. The state had provided the tools and charted
the course, and the small holders through their own efforts
were using the tools to gain their livelihood. Again, the emphasis was being put on *help to self-help*. Dr. Willandt has
expressed in a study of the Finnish small holder this point of

view: "The most important act of the Finnish government has been the liberating of the tenant farmer. . . . In depressed periods of agriculture when prices decline it is more critical for large estates than for the small holder who is in a more flexible position. Large and middle-sized farms are considered as business enterprises where the highest possible return on the capital invested must be obtained. But the small farm holdings cannot be put in the category of businesses which strive for the highest possible economic return. Instead, they have to be thought of in the light of a home and working place for the small farmer and his family, in which all the members of the family are working together to the best of their strength and ability to gain a living." *

RESETTLEMENT IN NORWAY

Three main classes of society existed in the early periods of Norwegian history: the jarl, the carl, and the thrall. The jarl was the militarist, responsible for the aggressions of the Viking age. He acquired land for the prestige it conferred upon him rather than from any interest in cultivation. The thralls, as a class, were mainly drawn from the captives secured in early Viking raids. They were bound to the land and were the cultivators of the soil. The effect of Christianity brought some degree of emancipation, but, bound to one spot by possessing a dwelling in return for work done for the owner of the estate, the liberated thrall lived in a condition of partial servitude. As a landless tenant he inherited much of the contempt accorded to the early thrall. Frustration of the desire of this laboring group to become owners of the holdings they occupied brought a sense of social inferiority and laid the basis for widespread unrest and later political action. By the middle of

---

* O. W. Willandt, *Suomen Peinviljelijain Taloudesta* ("The Economic Conditions of Finland's Small Farmers"), Economic Advisory Council, Helsinki, 1928. (Translated from the Finnish.)

the seventeenth century, tenants outnumbered owners two to one, and the principal grievances constituted the inability of these tenants to obtain long leases and the extortionate rents which were charged them.

The oppression of the landless tenants was lifted by the Treaty of Copenhagen in 1660 when the landowning nobles were overthrown and the Norwegians were freed from the class which had dominated them. The impoverished Frederick III in 1661 decreed an extensive sale of crown property and Norwegian tenant farmers began to purchase holdings. Also, because of the decree taxing large estates and consequently making them unprofitable, the estate owners began to sell land to their tenants. Over the centuries the trend from leasehold to ownership continued. In modern times this movement received its greatest acceleration from conditions brought about by the World War. In the war period and after, partly owing to the need for increased food production and partly to satisfy the social needs, steps were taken both to increase the number of persons on agricultural holdings and to improve rural living conditions. Extensive colonization measures were adopted in 1920 by Parliament and these, with subsequent alterations, instituted the present program.

In Norway the geographical and climatic factors have combined to make the lot of the farmer one which calls for exceptional courage and patience. Seventy per cent of the country's area, consisting of mountain ranges and lakes, is uncultivable; half the country in its northern reaches falls within the Arctic region. The ground is steeply rolling, and because of glacial deposit most of it is difficult to plow, but when once brought under cultivation it is very productive. A short growing season adds a further handicap. Despite these hardships, agriculture engages 35 per cent of the country's total population, many of whom combine summer farming with winter forestry or, to a lesser degree, with fishing. In general, agricultural methods are progressive and modern equipment is found on even the small farms.

Norway today is a country of small independent farms. As a matter of fact, of the some 142,690 separate holdings only 21 properties contain more than 250 acres of cultivated land. The average holding consists of slightly over 7 acres. Most of the farms, however, possess additional stretches of forest, grassland, or mountain pasture which contribute considerably to the farmers' incomes. It is estimated by the state that 85 per cent of the agricultural population are owners of their own farms while 14.3 per cent cultivate leased land. The policy of Norway has not only embraced the substitution of ownership for tenancy but it has given equal importance to making available to each generation of agricultural youth the opportunity to become established on farms, thus maintaining the tradition of independence.

Under the terms of the colonization law of 1920 as now in effect, the country is divided into eighteen rural districts with two additional municipal districts. The council in each district elects a land committee composed of five members whose names have been proposed by local associations of farmers, including the small holders. This land committee then engages one or, if necessary, several persons to plan and execute the colonization work in the district. One half of all expenses connected with the operation of the land committee is met by the state, one fourth by the county, and the remaining one fourth by the local district itself. These committees function under and co-operate with the central "New Cultivation" office in the state's department of agriculture.

Land for new small holdings is secured from state-owned property, from that held by the county agricultural societies, from that bought up by colonization associations, and from private sources. The agricultural societies and those colonization associations recognized as having a social purpose * may secure direct loans from the state for the purchase of arable land to be distributed to applicants for small holdings. These loans are exempt from interest payment for a period of five years, and, further, the state waives the demand for repayment on any difference between the price paid for the land by the distributing agency and that received from the small holder. Other colonization associations of a private character cannot secure the same liberal terms. In all cases, land for colonization purposes is bought at the market price. The state holds the right of expropriation but this power has seldom been exercised. Land acquired by the different agencies is divided into holdings suitable in size for the district and sold to the applicants at a low cost.

In the colonization program an applicant may secure funds not only for the acquisition of land but also for the erection of buildings and for cultivation. The maximum amount the state will advance for the land is about $1,875, with the stipulation that the holding must not be less than seven and one half acres. No interest is required to be paid on the loan for the first seven years and after that the interest rate is 4 per cent annually for a total of forty-two years, dating from the advancement of the loan. The small holder may not sell his property within the first ten years without permission of the government. On the other hand, he is allowed to increase the size of the holding as he wishes on his own responsibility. Because of the watchful eye of the state over a small holder's property, the element of speculation is practically eliminated.

Concerning the erection of buildings, the state makes a

---

* One of the outstanding colonization associations is "Nyjord," founded in 1908 with the purpose of combating excessive emigration to foreign countries as well as to give guidance to returning settlers. The association is directly concerned with colonization work. The chief source of its operating funds in recent years has been the state, an instance of the state's desire to accelerate the program.

maximum outright grant to the applicant of $450 for the out-buildings and a maximum of $125 for the dwelling. For the initial costs of cultivating the land the state makes an outright grant of 22 per cent of its estimated cost with a set limit and extends a Land Cultivation Loan at the interest rate of 2½ per cent a year. This loan is exempt from repayment for the first five years and is thereafter repayable during the following fif-teen years. The maximum amount of this loan to a small holder is limited to $1,250. The maximum appropriation to a small holder applicant for land, buildings, and cultivation may not exceed a sum of $4,000. The state has set up a special Bank for Small Holders for financing loans of this kind.

An applicant for state assistance in securing a small holding must be at least twenty-one years of age and not over sixty-five years of age. He must give reasonable indication that he can provide for his family on a holding if given opportunity. To be eligible he must not possess personal means exceeding about $1,800 nor have an annual income of more than $625. Although the applicant does not necessarily have to possess any personal means at all to secure a holding, and in many cases small farms have been allotted to persons in this condi-tion, the state considers it desirable for the applicant to have about $250 in cash or credit.

In establishing the small farmer on a new holding the state makes available designs and plans of dwelling houses and barns; architectural service is engaged to prepare stock plans from which the applicant can select the type of buildings best suited to his needs, subject to the approval of the local com-mittee. If he engages his own builder, the construction work is supervised by the office of the local committee. The usual type of dwelling house is generally similar to that used in Sweden, perhaps even more simplified.

Through colonization activities, between the years 1921 and 1936 the state has given assistance, either directly or through the colonization societies, toward the establishment of some eleven thousand independent small holdings; the program progressing at the present rate of about two thousand new holdings a year. Most of the settlers on these small holdings were originally farm laborers and the sons of farmers, foresters, or fishermen. The average small holder possesses in farm livestock a horse, one or two cows depending on his milk sale, a pig for his own use, and sheep in the mountain sections. The approximate net income of the Norwegian small holder is from $150 to $300 a year, derived chiefly from milk, eggs, chickens, potatoes, pigs, and silver foxes—the milk and silver foxes being the two largest single items. Some holdings market vegetables but these are limited to locations near towns. During the winter season timber provides a part of the income for holdings in forest districts. Also, handicraft is a source of income, the government assisting in marketing the finished products by maintaining a handicraft center in Oslo. In this way native craftsmanship is being nationally encouraged.

Co-operative societies in Norway have been forced to overcome severe obstacles. The physical conditions of the country with scattered settlements and difficult communication have made co-operative activity complicated; and, too, legislation designed to prevent the formation of monopolies has restricted the ready expansion of closely knit co-operative organizations. Nevertheless, the co-operative movement has shown an extensive development in recent years, and while not yet comparable to that in Denmark, Sweden, and Finland it has drilled deep roots into Norwegian soil and is growing steadily. Although in Norway the percentage of membership in relation to the whole population ranks fourth in place among the Scandinavian countries, the turn-over in consumer goods per member is highest. Independent small farmers account for 26.3 per cent of the total membership in the co-operative societies, which operate some 800 stores. Local societies are members of the Norges Kooperative Landsforening (the Co-operative Union and Wholesale Society of Norway), which operates 171 production centers and makes commodities of good quality available at a low price. Among the organizations for marketing the products of the small farms are 500 cooperative creameries and many egg centrals; there are also special societies with over 2,000 branches which handle farm supplies.

The brilliant contributions to literature made by Norwegian writers is a reflection of the high standard of education among the people. The ability to read and write in the mother tongue is possessed by practically all the Norwegian people. Even the small farmer is fond of reading and interests himself in political and social questions. Besides the agricultural schools in the rural sections, the government conducts a State Training School for Teachers to Small Holders and in addition contributes three quarters of the expense of operating seven schools for small holders located in various parts of the country. The course of instruction in the State Training School for Teachers includes general agricultural subjects, but the emphasis is put on the teaching of such minor agricultural industries as gardening, raising of small domestic animals, fish-hatching, and home industries, which are of special importance to the small holder. In the seven schools for small holders, instruction centers around handicraft, gardening, and the raising of pigs, poultry, rabbits, and bees. Each of these schools conducts a demonstration small holding which is operated by the students. An applicant for a small holding or any young farmer desiring to better equip himself may enroll in these small holder schools for terms of from six months to a year. As the state provides free scholarship, the expense is negligible. Ages of students range from eighteen to twenty-four years. Another form of instruction for the small holder is

the yearly tour of small holders, toward the expenses of which
the state makes a contribution.

A number of state-assisted small holdings are located in the
neighborhood of the Hvam school for small holders near
Arnes. We went by train to see the school and colony. The
first of these holdings, now comprising a group of fifteen, was
established over a decade ago. Asking Mr. Johannes Joie, as-
sistant-director of the school, what proportion of the fifteen
farmers had proved successful he lightly replied, "All but one
small holder, and he runs around the country with his truck
doing everything but look after his own place!" Mr. Joie also
commented that the position of the small holder was most advantageous when he had a number of products to market
rather than being compelled to rely on one or two.

Of a number of these small holdings visited, one stood out
particularly as seeming to symbolize the value of the state's
program in aiding a Norwegian farm family. Three generations lived on this small farm and their livelihood was gained
from it. Through state aid the family had been enabled to
move from poor agricultural land in another district to this
section where the soil was good. In the grandfather, a tall,
well-built man with a dark beard, one saw a hereditary strain
of the dauntless Vikings. His stalwart son, a few inches taller,
farmed the holding with him. The son's wife and three tow-
headed healthy children made up the household. The holding had been acquired through the state's colonization program twelve years before. Of the fifty acres in this holding
about half were under cultivation and the other half in forest land. The family's net income was about $370 a year and
was derived from the sale of potatoes, milk, vegetables, timber, and silver foxes. Their livestock consisted of six cows, a
calf, a horse, two pigs (although they occasionally had as
many as twenty), and some chickens. In addition there were
seven silver foxes. The products were disposed of through the

local co-operative creamery and through private markets. They purchased their farm supplies from a co-operative group of farmers. It was interesting to hear from the tall son that he had attended a small holder school and that both he and his father had gone on small holder tours in the summer.

The dwelling house was a substantial two-story frame building painted red with white trimmings and resting on a concrete foundation. The water supply came from a well outside the house and there was a pipe line to the barn. Heating was done by room stoves using wood as fuel. Electricity was not at hand, but the family expected the line to be brought in shortly by the county-owned electrical plant. The grandfather reported that in addition to the interest paid on the colonization loan from the state, they paid local taxes amounting to about $27 a year, and because their net income was less than $500, they were not required to pay any income tax. In leaving, the grandfather expressed a deep appreciation of what the state had done for him, saying "I had two sons who planned to emigrate to the United States, but because of the government's colonization program, which gave them an opportunity to obtain a living here on the land, they did not have to go. . . . Without the government's help these little farms could not have been."

The Norwegian plan for better rural housing and living is based on the principle that prevention is easier than cure. In a country where neither the national resources nor the means of making a living are abundant, the Norwegians consider that an agricultural population on independent holdings, adequately housed and modernly equipped, is vital to the welfare of the country. And this colonization program has won the acclaim of the people. As stated to me by one of the government's officials, "Nothing has been as popular as this movement with the people." The Norwegians love their land and, too, they love their independence. Combine the two and we

get that beautiful passage from one of Norway's great writers,
Knut Hamsun:

"Look at you folk at Sellanraa, now; looking up at blue
peaks every day of your lives; no new-fangled inventions
about that, but field and rocky peaks, rooted deep in the past
—but you've them for companionship. They you are, living in
touch with heaven and earth, one with them, one with all
these wide deep-rooted things. No need of a sword in your
hands, you go through life bareheaded, barehanded, in the
midst of a great kindliness. Look, Nature's there, for you and
yours to have and enjoy. Man and Nature don't bombard each
other, but agree; they don't compete, race one against another, but go together. There's you Sellanraa folk, in all this,
living there. Field and forest, moors and meadow, and sky
and stars—oh, 'tis not poor and sparingly counted out, but
without measure.

"Listen to me, Sivert; you be content! You've everything to
live on, everything to live for, everything to believe in; being
born and bringing forth, you are the needful on earth. 'Tis not
all that are so, but you are so; needful on earth. 'Tis you that
maintain life. Generation to generation, breeding ever anew;
and when you die, the new stock goes on. That's the meaning
of eternal life. What you get out of it? Nothing can put you
under orders and lord it over you Sellanraa folk, you've peace
and authority and this great kindliness all round. That's what
you get for it." *

---

* *Growth of the Soil* (New York: Alfred A. Knopf, and Copenhagen:
Gyldendalske Goghandel Nordisk Forlag). Reprinted with the special permission of these publishers.

DENMARK

The dwelling on a small state-assisted holding

A small holder in front of his substantial brick barn with thatched roof, near Spanager

A forest subsistence holding

SWEDEN

A small farm holding under the Swedish "Own Homes" program

FINLAND

A small holding, with t[...] bathhouse at the right of t[...] picture and "Finnish cotto[...] drying in the foreground

NORWAY

A small holding under t[...] Norwegian program

NORWAY

Three generations of a N[...] wegian family on a small hol[...] ing

NORWAY

The school for small ho[...] ers at Hvam. Each one of t[...] seven schools of this ki[...] conducts a demonstrat[...] small holding operated [...] the students

5. APPLIED PHILOSOPHY

CALDERON IN ONE OF HIS CHARMING COMEDIES says, "A man who has never seen the sun cannot be blamed for thinking that no glory can exceed that of the moon. A man who has seen neither moon nor sun cannot be blamed for talking of the unrivaled brightness of the morning star." While one does not expect to find perfection in any system of government, it is impossible to view the Scandinavian scene without appreciating the realistic and effective way in which many social problems have been met; especially is this true in urban and rural housing. However, it is not the purpose here to formulate a program for the United States based on Scandinavian experience—that would be an impertinence. Rather, it is to make a few observations upon common problems.

As has been seen, the basis of a comprehensive housing program rests on a satisfactory solution of the land question; and in urban areas, where unbridled speculation brings high land costs, the only escape short of drastic means is through the purchase of land by government agencies at market prices in advance of the need. It has been shown that this responsibility can be appropriately delegated to the municipalities, as evidenced in Copenhagen, Stockholm, Helsinki, and some of the other cities. While the initial expense of this activity requires funds or credit, the actual savings and advantages have made it a thoroughly practical undertaking.

Government intervention in meeting the housing needs

brought a general improvement in the quality of dwellings erected. In extending financial aid, making cheap land available, and exempting taxes under certain limitations, this public support was conditioned on the observance of certain minimum standards of health and comfort which had the effect of raising general housing standards. Public housing threw down a challenge which private industry accepted by raising its own standards—an important effect of public housing.

Why should standards be set? Why should slums be cleared and replaced with better housing? Let us take the actual case of Dominick Guariglia, a case not uncommon in the slums. Ten years ago the White Door Settlement in the lower east side of New York selected Dominick, aged nine, as a typical underprivileged child, and, using his picture on a blotter, an appeal was made to give such youngsters a chance. But little came from the appeal. A few months ago a New York daily carried the tragic headline that the same Dominick, now nineteen, had been sentenced to die in the electric chair for the murder of a detective in a tearoom holdup. A probation report told this pathetic story: "He was reared in a congested tenement where, during the formative years, he came into contact with demoralizing neighborhood influences . . . spent most of his time in pool-rooms . . . parents too busy with their economic problems to give him any individual attention. . . ." The report concludes with the statement that "Dominick never had a chance!" And, the Dominicks of the slums never will have a chance unless their environment is changed by decent housing conditions. As the London County Council expresses it, "The health of the community depends on the health of the individual who is in turn dependent on his environment. There is nothing in the nature of things to prevent that environment being adjusted within limits in accordance with the wishes of mankind."

The one and only reason why public aid is necessary for rehousing families in the slums is because private industry has not found it profitable to do so. Thus, the responsibility is left on the shoulders of public agencies. Today it is not a question whether a country can afford to bring decent housing within the reach of the low income groups but, instead, whether it can afford *not* to do so. Overcrowding of our slums leads to overcrowding of our jails, hospitals, and insane asylums. Therefore if the choice is to be made between relieving the overcrowding at one end or the other, it would be cheaper to society and certainly more humane to do the rebuilding in the slums. Looking at world conditions, Harold Butler, past director of the International Labor Office in Geneva, emphatically declares that "the very security of the State is now seen to depend not only on the inviolability of its frontiers but upon its ability to provide an orderly and sufficient existence to all its citizens." Surely the Dominicks of the slums are to be included in "all its citizens."

The Scandinavian governments believe that social housing calls for the active intervention of both national and municipal agencies on a partnership basis. It is not logical to think that we can develop a public housing program in the United States commensurate with the large and diversified needs unless federal, state, and municipal governments are each willing to assume an equitable share of assistance, both legislative and financial.

As noted, co-operative and public utility housing societies have been extensively developed in Scandinavia, receiving government aid in various forms. This housing, in its rent level one step above the subsidized municipal housing, fills the large gap which lies between the municipal housing and the housing produced by private initiative. But in the United States this gap has not been filled. A great mass of industrial and other urban workers are ineligible for public housing projects constructed under the United States Housing Act, because their incomes are slightly above the established maximum limits. On the other hand they cannot afford the rents asked for suitable private housing. They are the lost battalion in the housing field. To meet this pressing need funds should be established by the federal government or the states, or by both, from which loans could be secured at an interest rate low enough to enable these workers to form co-operative and limited dividend societies for meeting their own housing requirements. By appropriate legislative action, New York state has recently embarked on such a program.

In Scandinavia as in England, government aid to housing has in no way diminished private enterprise. As a matter of fact, a tremendous increase in private construction accompanied the public work. The reason this occurred was simple. When no-standard housing as exists in the slums is replaced by a condition embodying standards as found in public projects, the results are that private enterprise strives to further improve its own construction and to take advantage of the reclaimed neighborhood by erecting private projects. As an example of the latter, private builders constructed new housing adjacent to a large public housing project in Washington, D. C., because they recognized the value of the improved neighborhood.

Rural housing in Scandinavia has been shown to be inseparably identified with the extraordinary growth of independent small farm holdings. Since the problem of improving rural housing conditions bears directly on agricultural living and income it is felt that there is little use in adding to the indebtedness of the man on the land by furnishing him with either a new dwelling or improvements to an old one unless conditions are reasonably favorable for his being able to maintain himself on the holding. The foundation of these programs has been the replacement of tenancy by ownership.

The very forces which brought impoverishment and distress

to the formerly landless population in the Scandinavian countries are insidiously operating in the United States today. For
instance, take the Great Plains area: A recent government
survey shows that absentee ownership, the development of
the land in uneconomical units, and a predominating tenancy
have all become characteristics of this region; and, further,
that speculation raised the price of land far above its earning
value, a condition intensified by an oppressive credit system.
Consequently a large part of the land has now fallen into the
hands of banks and other lending agencies, and an excessive
number of owners have lost their farms through tax sales,
mortgage foreclosures, and bankruptcies. The survey adds
that "It has been difficult enough in the past for a young man
to climb the ladder from hired man to tenant to owner of a
farm; today except under the most favorable circumstances it
is well nigh impossible." A serious indictment of the present
situation.

Erskine Caldwell sharply etches the wretchedness of tenant
farmers in the deep South: "Hundreds of communities in
Georgia, Alabama, Mississippi, and Arkansas exist without
roads, and travel is done across creeks without bridges, fields
without so much as a cow path. These are the unknown people of today; the tenant farmers of the South. These are the
people who hide their nakedness behind trees when a stranger
wanders off the main traveled roads. Here are the deformed
starved children born since 1929. Here are the men who strip
leaves off trees, dig roots out of the earth, and snare whatever
wild animal they can. . . . There is hunger in their eyes as
well as in their bellies. They grasp for a word of hope. They
plead for a word of advice. They have no friend or leader to
help them."

Tenancy existing within families, as in the case of a son
renting a farm from an aging father or relative, is not an evil.
But where tenancy represents a hopeless treadmill of insecure

tenure and less than subsistence income, it becomes a serious national problem which cannot be ignored. And to further complicate the situation in this country, the growth of large scale corporation farming has intensified seasonal employment. Thousands of agricultural laborers drift from place to place harvesting short-season crops. This industrialized agriculture has also brought a deadly competition which small farmers find well nigh impossible to meet. One such large industrial farm in New Jersey, for instance, can produce cabbages at a cost of one cent a head while it costs the small farmers in the same neighborhood from four to five cents. From a distracted farm woman in Minnesota came this letter appearing in the *Farmer's Wife* magazine: "Dear Editor— My husband is a good farmer and we have one son at home. We would be classed with 'small farmers' and find it hard— as so many others do—to rent a good farm. The big farmers are crowding us out. Is it fair for one man to rent and operate six to eight hundred acres just because he owns tractors and equipment to farm it, forcing the small farmer to sell out, move to town, and work at whatever he can get—or go on relief? What about our boys? Will times ever change back, so that we may have a chance again?—From a Worried Mother."

If it were possible to generalize we might say that the deliberate intent of the Scandinavian democracies to promote the welfare of their rural populations takes the form of a three-point program. One, the creation of independently owned, family-sized holdings for full or part-time agricultural purposes through state assistance and guidance. Two, the extension of adult education in people's colleges and small holder schools. Three, an encouragement in the wide use of producer and consumer co-operatives. Points two and three are considered essential to the maintenance of the small holder on his holding, thus implementing point one.

The philosophy behind rural small holdings may be said to

be based on the premise that land characterized by small units and cultivated independently is more beneficial to society as a whole than land held predominately in large units cultivated under a system of tenancy or hired labor. William James expresses the kernel of this philosophy in one of his letters, "As for me, my bed is made: I am against bigness and greatness in all their forms. . . . I am against big successes and big results; and in favour of the eternal forces of truth which always work in the individual."

A philosophy of this kind harnessed to the experience of Scandinavia serves to check the trend toward large industrialized farm units, wherein fewer and fewer people wield the producing power leaving ever increasing numbers of landless farm families thrown like chaff from the machine. Symbolic of the system, John Steinbeck vividly describes the supplanting of independent farmers by the employee mechanic who drives the tractor down the long cotton rows: "He loved the land no more than the bank loved the land. He could admire the tractor—its machined surfaces, its surge of power, the roar of its detonating cylinders; but it was not his tractor. Behind the tractor rolled the shining disks, cutting the earth with blades. . . . The driver sat in his iron seat and he was proud of the straight lines he did not will, proud of the tractor he did not own or love, proud of the power he could not control. And when that crop grew, and was harvested, no man had crumpled a hot clod in his fingers and let the earth sift past his fingertips. No man had touched the seed, or lusted for the growth. The land bore under iron, and under iron gradually died; for it was not loved or hated, it had no prayers or curses." *

The simple logic of the small holder movement is abiding and easily understood. In the four Scandinavian countries the

---

* John Steinbeck, *Grapes of Wrath* (New York, The Viking Press, 1939). Reprinted with special permission of the publishers.

program is marked by the government's sympathetic interest and inclination to provide the essentials of production for a good life in a rural environment. In both rural and urban areas the recurring theme running through social undertakings, including housing, is *help to self-help*.

With its bearing on a progressing democracy, we in the United States can fittingly appropriate the lofty thought of our own Oliver Wendell Holmes, "I find that the great thing in this life is not where we stand but in what direction we are moving."

INDEX

INDEX